THE BEST IS YET TO COME

DR. ANTHONY J. WIGGINS

Published by Book Writing Pioneer

Cover design by Book Writing Pioneer

ISBN: Printed in the United States

TABLE OF CONTENTS

Introduction

It may seem somewhat strange to say, but I truly thank and praise God for the fact that I was not born with what is known as a **"proverbial gold spoon in my mouth."** However, I know quite a few people who were, but that's another story for another time. Because God is exactly who and what He says that He is, I have what I have, and I am what I am—nothing more than a sinner saved by His grace alone! No more, no less! This fact is simply amazing to me!

I can only imagine how hard and how difficult it was, is, and has been to measure my success against the success of those who were born into a family with a background of great affluence, influence, popularity, and success, as opposed to that of someone (like myself) who only by the grace of God has been able to transform his life from literally and figuratively "rags" to the narrative of a "rags-to-riches" story.

The truth be told, I didn't exactly come from "rags," and the only "riches" that I have or possess are through and because of Jesus Christ! His presence alone in my life has made the difference in who and what I am today—a child of God!

The Bible is resplendent with an amazing array of accounts of the lives of many such people. Personally, I can both relate to and appreciate how the hand of God has majestically moved within, touched, and done that which only God Himself could do in the lives of what the world views as just plain old ordinary people—like me, my family in particular, and probably many of you reading this book.

These are the people that God, by and large, chooses to use as an example to prove for all to witness just what His omnipotent power, love, mercy, and grace alone can accomplish in their lives—if they are committed to living for Him and serving Him unconditionally.

One of the most famous of all the rags-to-riches stories found in the Bible focuses on the life of Joseph (Genesis chapter 37). Joseph was the "most beloved" of his father Jacob's twelve sons, and in fact, he received special favors and privileges from his father simply because he was born during the time of Jacob's old age. Though Jacob loved all his children, he did not hide the fact of his "special preferred love" for his son Joseph, and because of this, Joseph's eleven brothers hated him.

The hatred and the animosity that Joseph's brothers had for him eventually boiled over one day to the point that when they (his brothers) had an opportunity to rid him from their lives for what they thought would be forever, they conspired and engaged in a plan to sell him into slavery to a group of Midianite merchants for, ironically, twenty shekels (pieces of silver—Genesis 37:20), the going rate for the "cost" of a slave, which equated to the thirty pieces of silver that Jesus Himself was sold for in Matthew 27:3 by Judas (also see Exodus 21:28–32).

This was the beginning of Joseph's rags-to-riches story, which began with him being the "beloved son" of his father Jacob, hated by his brothers, and sold by them into the confinement of a "pit," and then into slavery in Egypt. Joseph's story saw him transition from a "preferred" place of honor in his father Jacob's house to slavery in Egypt and prison, only to ultimately find favor in the eyes of God and rise to become the Governor of Egypt! (Genesis 42). Because of the hand of God on his life, Joseph's latter days became greater than his former days (Haggai 2:9, Job 8:7).

If we remain faithful in our commitment to honor and to serve God, the same blessing will come our way, and we will experience the mighty hand of God working in a way that we could never even begin to imagine or understand!

Again, our Lord and Savior Jesus Christ's story "began" in heaven as the only begotten beloved Son of God Himself, allowed by God the Father to become "draped" in sin and shame—fashioned in the form of a man (John 1:14)—come down to a sin-filled world to die on the cross for our sins, to be sold by His "brother" Judas (Matthew 26:14–16), and after being resurrected from the grave, ascended to the place of honor and glory at the right hand of God in heaven! (Matthew chapter 28, Acts chapters 1 and 2).

Recently, in a conversation with my "oldest aunt" (Mary Ballentine), I couldn't resist the opportunity to ask her about the "humble" beginnings of our Wiggins family, which I have always been told began in the "red hills" of Decatur, Alabama. After a few silent moments of what I believe were deep, reflective thoughts and somber pondering, Aunt Mary recounted these words about some of the history of our family that she experienced in her childhood and early life:

"Growing up in a family of ten brothers and sisters (eleven counting herself), we didn't have much, but God blessed us in such a way that we always had food to eat, a set of clean clothes to wear, and a warm place to lay our heads down at night. Mom and Dad (my grandparents, Mary and James Wiggins) always worked hard and sacrificed a lot for us to have the necessities of life, but it was the prayers of a praying mother (Mom was a woman of faith and prayer) that sustained us through those challenging times. Without those prayers that 'Mom' prayed, we would have never made it."

"We had more than some and not as much as others. We lived a simple but modest lifestyle, filled with the love and the support of family togetherness—tempered and held together by the love of God. What more could we possibly need or want?"

"Though Dad (my grandfather) was uneducated and not able to read or write anything except his name, he was able to build a house with his own hands, and Mom turned it into a loving home for all of us. Truly, God has sustained us, ordered our steps, and directed our paths as a family! For that, I am eternally grateful!"

What a great legacy of faith and trust in God my family had and still has today! I, along with my brothers, my sisters, and my cousins, am living proof of the faithfulness and the goodness of God.

In my way of thinking, my family's "small and humble beginnings" reflected in the eighth chapter of Job, verse 7, have been a precursor signaling the fact that by the grace of God, we can bear witness that our "latter days" (my family's) in fact even continue today to be greater than our former ones. This truth has unfolded itself before my very eyes, and I am a living witness!

I personally can remember growing up and sharing not only one bedroom with three brothers and a cousin (five of us in one bedroom) but also wearing the same clothes! No, we weren't "poor," but we were taught to do that which we needed to do to survive—and we did because we knew that the presence of God and His hand on us was paramount in our lives, and it has made a significant difference in where we as a family are today.

Yes, this modest "snippet" of my life is just a chronicle of some of my early (former) days and that of my family. Many more similar stories exist, but I will always remember that when you trust and believe in God by faith, the best is yet to come!

My grandmother (Mary Wiggins) prayed, and God is still answering her prayers for our family today! I thank and praise God that I had the opportunity (as a child, a teenager, and an adult) to be in her presence firsthand to witness the prayer life of the amazing woman of God that she (my grandmother) was.

For one, my very life and the success that I have gained are evidence. It is true that the effectual fervent prayers of the righteous will indeed avail much (James 5:16)! My grandmother, if nothing else, was certainly a righteous woman of faith, and her prayer life revealed this truth! Her commitment to prayer for her family has "paid dividends!" My life itself speaks volumes for this fact and is Exhibit Number One!

As I look at what now are my "latter days," all I can say is look at God, all that He has done, and all that He is going to do! Little becomes much, and less becomes greater when placed in His hands!

From the modest and humble beginnings of my family—which I am not too ashamed to mention included a grandfather (James Wiggins) who couldn't read or write—today, the legacy of my family (by the grace of God) proudly includes my brother Rod, a retired United States Army Captain; his daughter and son-in-law, PhDs of Clinical Psychology—Dan and Crystal Newman (both on staff at the University of Illinois); Valencia Wiggins, my "first cousin" (on staff at the Moody Bible Institute in Chicago, Illinois); myself, a Doctor of Theology, a high school educator, a hospice chaplain, and a pastor; Marcellus Wiggins, my young cousin who is an aspiring young medical doctor (a student) at Case Western Reserve University in Cleveland, Ohio; and Byron Davis, one of the first African-American Olympian swimmers, and his wife Annett, an Olympian volleyball player! All are committed, dedicated believers and followers of Jesus Christ and are strong witnesses for Him by and through their lives! Not by power, not by might, but by My Spirit, says the Lord! (Zechariah 4:6)

Truly, as a family, we have come this far (a long way) by faith—leaning, trusting, depending, and believing in God. There is no way we could have made it this far but for the hand of God ordering our steps, directing our paths, and opening closed doors on our behalf as only He could do—and has done.

He has never failed us yet, and **the best is still yet to come**! It is to this end that I would like to dedicate this book to my entire Wiggins family, too numerous to name individually, but I thank and praise God for each of you collectively as a group. Truly, as a family, we have come this far by faith, and especially to my wife Valerie, for her steadfast love and support for me throughout the best and the worst of times that we have experienced together, weathering the storms of life by the grace of God; to Sgt. Jeff Flaig, our "casualty officer" whose physical and emotional support for my family during the darkest days of our lives amidst the loss of our son Michael in the Iraq War in 2007, forever remains a constant reminder that **the best is still yet to come**; as well as to anyone and everyone who has come from small, humble, modest beginnings of their former days to a place today that we together can proudly celebrate and rejoice in the goodness of a God who continuously hears and answers our prayers. He may not come when we want Him, but we know that He is and always will be on time when He comes to see about resolving the issues of our lives and meeting our individual and specific needs according to His will. He has always done just that for me and my family.

"Though your beginnings will seem small, so prosperous will your future be." (**Job** 8:7, NIV) Rest assured and believe that by faith in God, the **best is yet to come** when His hands are touching your life—ordering, directing, and guiding your every step…

Chapter One
"Humble Beginnings"

"Your beginnings will seem humble, so prosperous will your future be."
(Job 8:7, NIV)

Whether or not a person succeeds in life should never be determined by how or where their lives started out, but rather it should be judged by how far they have come—and how far they can eventually go, trusting in the power of God for direction. According to the late Napoleon Hill, who was an American author, a journalist, and a noted salesman, "The road to success is paved with small beginnings." No matter how small those beginnings were or might have been, they have no real bearing upon whether any person is going to be successful in their lives.

Of the many books that Hill published promoting the principles of success, his two classic books (*The Law of Success*, published in 1928, and *Think and Grow Rich*, published in 1937) were and remain highly popular even today. The term "humble beginnings" is a phrase that reflects the modest yet unassuming start of someone or something before they "arrive" or become successful.

A deeper study and a reflective view of Job 8:7 seem to suggest to us that it is God's intention to bless Job with success and popularity after he has undergone a time of suffering, which we all are going to experience at some point in our lives.

No, Job's life didn't necessarily start out in or with humble beginnings, as the Bible describes him as a man of great integrity and wealth (Job chapter 1).

Job spent a great amount of his time before the presence of the Lord, praying on behalf of all his family, each day (seven sons, three daughters), if they "forgot" or neglected to pray for themselves. There was a day (I believe just like today with you and me) when Satan himself came before the presence of God, questioning and challenging the level and the magnitude of Job's faith in God. He still operates in much the same manner today.

God ultimately permitted Satan to put Job's faith in Him (God) to a test: "You can take everything away from My servant Job and all that he has, only you can't take his life" (Job 1:8–12). God alone has divine control and authority over anything and anyone that would dare to raise even a finger against us, His children! (Isaiah 54:17, "No weapon formed against us shall prosper!")

During Job's time of "testing" by God and "tempting" by Satan, he (Job) lost everything that he owned in the matter of just a few hours (Job chapter 1). Stripped naked and bare by the permissive, providential will of God, Job finds himself in a place and a time of having "nothing." (If you haven't been there, at some point in your life you will.)

At this difficult point in his life, Job chose "not to curse God" as Satan had predicted that he would, but rather he chose to bless His Name instead (Job 1:21–22): "The Lord gives and the Lord takes away, blessed be His Name!"

I believe that this phase of Job's life in some way reflects or speaks to the nature of his now "humble beginnings, or new beginnings." Job, like many of us today, went through (as we do today) and experienced a period in his life that included a great many personal, physical, emotional, and spiritual challenges and the testing of his faith in God by his wife, and even his three "best friends," who offered very little or no support for him during his weakest moments.

Because of the hand of God on his life and his faith in God, Job was able to maintain a form of positive trust in God's faithfulness (Job 13:15, "Though He slay me yet will I trust Him"), and if we fast forward to the time of his "latter days" (Job 42:10–17), we find that God blessed him with twice the abundance of what he possessed in his "former days!"

Not only did Job receive abundant physical blessings from God because he trusted in Him and never lost his faith, but God also "extended" his life another 140 years, and he was able to live to see his children as well as his grandchildren "grow up" (four generations) and leave them an inheritance! (Job 42:16)

One of the many lessons that I personally have learned from the life of Job, and that I can testify and witness on behalf of my entire Wiggins' family about, is that however and wherever our journey of life began (even with and in humble beginnings), we must never stop trusting in God and placing our confidence in Him. Everything that we have, ever hope to have, or even accomplished in life, is a gift from God!

Again, Job, like many of us even today, spent (and spends) a great amount of time, effort, and energy trying to understand just why it is that God allows "bad things to happen to good people." Unfortunately, we seem to forget that all of us are "sinners saved by the grace of God" (Romans 3:23), and therefore we should never think of ourselves as being "good" (Romans 3:10–12, Psalm 51:5).

According to Mark 10:18, "no one is good, except God alone." We as human beings were created to be good and to do good, but God created us with the mindset and the ability to have a "free choice."

Unfortunately, we refuse to embrace that which is "good" (holy) and embrace those things that arise out of our own sinful desires and lusts.

Even when we try to do good, evil is always present around, and within us, and amid our struggles, we choose to do that which is not right or good (Romans 7:21).

Consequently, even our modest humble beginnings at their best are rooted in sin, which is our nature from birth (see again Psalm 51:5).

In the presence and the light of others who always seemed to have more than I did in my "former days," to some degree, there was an element of shame associated with all the "things" that I didn't have simply because we couldn't afford them. We didn't have the best of things, but we always had more than enough.

However, one of the distinct blessings of my "former" days that is still true even in my present "latter days," was the fact that I was raised in a Christian home. I can proudly remember "going to church" all the time (every day and twice on Sundays!). The older I grew, the more I began to realize how significantly important this was and has been, as it helped to mold and to shape me into who and what I am today (a man of faith).

The blessing was the fact that not only were the godly principles of Jesus Christ taught to me from the Bible, but more importantly, these principles were modeled and lived out in front of me by everyone—Mom, Dad, grandparents, uncles, and aunts who played a meaningful role in my life. One of the most important of all the attributes of Jesus Christ that should be in the heart of every Christian is the importance of having and fostering a humble spirit.

One of the passages of Scripture from the Word of God that I learned as a child, which has perhaps impacted me the most, still speaks to me today about how we, as God's people, should present ourselves:

"Clothed in compassion, kindness, humility, gentleness, and patience." (Colossians 3:12) "Those who exalt themselves shall one day be humbled, and those who humble themselves shall one day be exalted."

For a Christian, "humility is fear of the Lord, which results in wages that are riches, honor, and life." (Proverbs 22:4)

The lifelong lesson learned (by me) is that there should not be any shame associated with our meager or humble beginnings because, from these beginnings, God can take that which is or seems to be ordinary in its "former days" and accomplish that which can become extraordinary in service and commitment to His kingdom in their latter days!

Now, considering all that I have learned and experienced in my life, I can proudly—and without shame—take a long, fresh, retrospective look back over the humble beginnings of my family and rejoice when I see, woven like a "seam of tapestry," the workings of the hand of Almighty God intricately weaving and shaping our lives into a beautiful work of art that bears witness and serves as a testimony to some of His greatest work! My family is not perfect, but we are and have been truly blessed. Certainly, God is good, and we are the recipients of His goodness!

Sir Francis Drake, a famous English explorer and one of the first men to circumnavigate the "known" world (1577–1580), coined the phrase: "Greatness comes from small or humble beginnings." Going a step further, I can only say that I don't know whether Drake himself was a believer or a follower of God through faith in Jesus Christ, but I do know and believe that if you (or anyone) commit yourself wholly, fully, and completely to following God, regardless of your beginnings, greatness can and will emerge if your efforts are devoted to serving Him unconditionally.

I love the NLT (New Living Translation) of 1 Corinthians 1:27: "Instead, God chose things the world considers foolish to shame those who think they are wise. And He chose things that are powerless to shame those who are powerful."

When I again look at my family, I think: what could be "more foolish" than to trace the humble beginnings of the patriarch of our family—my grandfather (James Wiggins), who couldn't read or write his own name in the "former days" of my family's history—to the present "latter days" of my family today, where you can "find" a host of successful, accomplished college graduates, and a few PhDs and doctors?

The Bible is full of men and women from simple, humble beginnings (namely, our Lord and Savior Jesus Christ Himself, Mary His mother, Ruth, Hannah, Moses, David, to name a few) who were, by the power of God, transformed into becoming examples and witnesses that anything is possible when God touches your life.

Personally, at this point in my life (73 years old), I am still in the position of receiving the present "latter-day" blessings of my life! God is still actively at work doing great things for me as I strive to remain open, available, and willing to follow in the direction that He is leading me. The best is yet to come!

Quite simply, these "latter days" that I am experiencing (now) have been and are the most exciting days of my life as I wait in prayerful anticipation and expectation for my "next assignment on this Christian journey of service and ministry!" What God has already done for me and what He is doing in my life presently is and has been simply amazing! It's humbling to think that He (God) has something special in store for me in terms of my commitment to follow Him.

Time after time (ironically, at the precise time I am writing this book), I find myself asking these questions: "Why is God choosing to call me from the humble beginnings of my 'former days' even to consider using me in a greater way for His honor and glory in my present latter days?"

God alone knows what He is doing, why He is doing it, and when He is going to do all that He promised me (or us) that He would do. I have learned (and am still learning) to wait in humble anticipation, expectation, and acceptance of His sovereign plan and will for my life!

My constant, consistent, and continuous prayer has always been that God would lead, guide, direct, and place me in the position that would best allow me to be used further to spread the message of the gospel of Jesus Christ. Ultimately, all I want to do is to please Him in all that I do with all the talent and the ability that He has given to me.

When I think about the humble beginnings of my life, I thank and praise God that I can draw encouragement as well as inspiration from the life of biblical characters like King David, whose extraordinary journey began as a lowly, humble shepherd boy and ended with him becoming the most revered King of Israel (1 Samuel chapters 16 and 17).

Like David, I have often felt and believed that for quite a "season" in my life of ministry, as well as my work for the Lord, I have labored in obscurity. That is not to say that the only reason that I work for the Lord is that I might be seen or recognized by others by having my work and efforts applauded. I fully understand and appreciate the fact that this life of ministry is not even about me.

One of the most significant and amazing facts about the life of David that has encouraged me is that while he labored in what was apparent anonymity in the fields as a shepherd boy tending his father's sheep, God saw in him what most others couldn't or didn't see—his level of commitment to the task that he was assigned to, regardless of how obscure it was.

Consequently, when the prophet Samuel came to Jesse's house (David's father) in search of the new prospective king of Israel that he had been chosen to anoint, Samuel's attention was drawn to that of David's older brother Eliab, who "had the appearance of a great leader" and probably was the obvious choice to become the next king.

1 Samuel 16:7 records God's response to Samuel's proposed decision: "Do not look at his countenance (or outward appearance) or the height of his stature because I do not see the way that man sees. I have rejected him because man only is concerned about the outward appearance, but God looks at the heart."

David's humble appearance and the fact that his "résumé" could only boast of him having only served as a shepherd boy revealed nothing about what God saw in his (David's) heart! David's story tells us that he didn't immediately become Israel's king, but he was anointed (as king) before he was appointed, and went back to laboring as a shepherd boy in his father's field!

For the past twenty years, I have labored tirelessly, as well as with a degree of relative anonymity, serving as the senior pastor and the founder of a small church (Friends Fellowship Bible Church, just under one hundred members) in Cleveland, Ohio.

The most invaluable lesson that I have learned from this humble yet important experience is that God has called us (me) to work for Him wherever it is that He places us, whether we ever receive the accolades, applause, recognition, or praises of men and women around us.

Being faithfully committed to Him is all that ultimately is going to matter on that day when we all stand before His presence—hopefully and prayerfully to hear Him say: "Well done, thou good and faithful servant!" (Matthew 25:21).

As the iconic song by recording artist Tasha Cobbs Leonard humbly yet unashamedly declares, "I'm so glad that He knows my name!"

Though no one else seems to care or even be concerned about "who I am, what I do, or what I have done or why I have done it," God not only sees, but He knows and understands the story of my life from my humble beginnings even up until this present time that I am still putting forth my best effort to serve Him and to advance the kingdom of God on earth as He has called me to do!

It is not always one's actions that prove or show how humble they are, but rather it is that which composes the character of their heart.

When a humble person puts their faith as well as their trust in God, it is no secret and of no consequence that they have the capacity as well as the ability to accomplish great things.

Just like David (in 1 Samuel 18:18–23), I have asked myself the question: "Who am I that You would consider me for such a position as the one to lead Your people?" Why is it that You would be willing to entrust me, one possessing little or seemingly no apparent skill but that of a committed faith in You (God) as the underlying and stabilizing force that inspires, encourages, and compels me to believe that I indeed have the capacity and the wherewithal to advance the kingdom of God through sharing and spreading the gospel of Jesus Christ to a lost and dying world?

Christ in me indeed is my eternal hope of glory in the belief that "I can do all things through Him (Jesus Christ) who gives me the necessary strength." (Philippians 4:13)

I fully realize that in and of myself, I cannot do anything, but supported and undergirded by the amazing power of God, the prospects of what I (and what you) can accomplish are endless. There is simply no limit to what the power of God can do when it is fully unleashed in our lives.

Truly, "eyes have not seen and neither have ears heard—nor has it yet entered into the hearts of anyone—ever conceived all that God has prepared for those who love and trust Him!" (1 Corinthians 2:9)

I am further encouraged as well as inspired by the Apostle Paul's declaration in Colossians 1:27, "that Christ in me is indeed my ultimate hope of glory." The fact that Jesus Christ dwells in me through His Holy Spirit, I have the confident expectation as well as the assurance that there is always going to be the presence of an "eternal hope" for the future resonating in me in terms of what I am going to be able to achieve and to accomplish one day for the glory of God alone.

This alone again is one of the most important things that both compel and continue to help me to keep my eyes on "the prize of the high calling of God in Jesus Christ" (Philippians 3:13).

Humility suggests and reminds us from the Word of God that the very eyes of God are focused upon the heart, the mind, and the character of those possessing humble spirits, and not only does He promise to offer them direction and guidance for their lives, but one day, because of their humility and willingness to serve Him, they will be exalted far above any level or degree that they might have ever imagined!

Finally, it is a blessing to both realize and understand that God knows and understands our beginning as well as our ending. He is the One who, in "eternity past" by His own predestined will alone, called each of us and appointed a specific time, a specific place, as well as a specific plan for exactly what it is that He wanted us to accomplish and to achieve in our lifetime of ministry for Him.

No longer do I have to feel or believe that "I missed out" on not being called, appointed, or selected to any position that I might have desired to have or wished to fulfill. I have learned that God is not obligated or bound to give or grant us the things that we want or the position that we desire to have unless it is the plan that He has for our lives in order that His purpose for us might best be fulfilled.

"What God has for me is for me," and regardless of just how insignificant or humble "my beginning" might have been, it doesn't really matter in the total scheme of God's plan and will for my life.

From one of my old instructors at the Moody Bible Institute in Akron, Ohio (which I attended and graduated from in 1988), I learned one of the keys to Christian contentment and the wisdom behind a unique paraphrase of Philippians 4:11–12, which says: "Not that I speak in respect of want, for I have learned, in whatever state I am, therewith to be content. I know both how to be abased, and I know how to abound: everywhere and in all things I am instructed both to be full and to be hungry, both to abound and to suffer need."

My personalized paraphrase of this passage of Scripture simply says to me: "Where He leads me, I will follow, and what He feeds me, I will swallow!" It is in me allowing "my will" to align itself up to, conform to, and accept the "will of God" that is going to dictate and convey to me all of what I need to be satisfied and content with the course and the direction of my life as God reveals it to me.

No longer will I have to sit back and wonder "why this and not that" as God meticulously unveils the plan that He has for me and my life as I accept His will and His direction (although sometimes reluctantly, with apprehension). I have found that the more I am willing to accept His plan as well as His purpose for my life unconditionally and not question Him about how, why, and when things will be accomplished, the smoother the transition will be. Consequently, the reward as a result will also be greater.

Ultimately, this journey of my life, as it relates to my service and my commitment to following Jesus Christ, is not even about me, my humble beginnings, or whether I am doing that which I want to do or doing exactly what I believe God has called me to do.

Our human nature is such that in our "flesh" we would rather serve the Lord in the light of the position where we can receive the accolades and the applause of people around us because they can "see" what we do, and "know our name" as a frame of reference for who we are, and what we have done ("He's the pastor of Great and Mighty Baptist Church with a membership of 2,000 people") as opposed to being virtually unknown ("He's the pastor of Nobody Baptist Church with a membership of less than 100 people").

Again, I have learned (and am still learning) to be content and satisfied with where God has both called and placed me to serve Him as long as I can continue to point to the message of the gospel of Jesus Christ as the only solution for a lost and dying world that is impoverished by sin and in need of God's saving grace!

I have been both intrigued as well as inspired and blessed by the 120-year life of Moses, as it presents itself in three distinct periods of 40-year intervals (Deuteronomy 34:7). It wasn't until Moses reached the age of eighty that God called him to lead His people (the children of Israel) out of bondage and captivity in Egypt (Exodus 7:7).

In the first forty years of Moses' life, we see him in Egypt learning invaluable lessons from his mother, and then learning all the skills and expertise needed to help rule Egypt. Amazingly, in the second forty-year period of Moses' life, we see him laboring and working as a lowly shepherd tending the sheep in Midian in his father-in-law's (Jethro's) field.

During this time of insignificant humble service, God taught Moses how to be patient and to place his trust in God alone. It was during this time that Moses (according to Numbers 12:3) became the "meekest man on the earth." Finally, at the age of eighty years old (what about retirement?), God called him for the most challenging and exciting adventure of his life—leading God's people out of the captivity and bondage of Egypt at the hand of Pharaoh.

Moses initially "balked" at the command or request of God to return to Egypt, confront Pharaoh, and tell him, "God said, let My people go." (Exodus 5:1). His "balking" was based upon his belief that he was simply not fully qualified or able to deliver God's message to such a formidable opponent as Pharaoh.

God's response to Moses then (Exodus 4:12: I will help you to speak, and tell you what to say") should be our battle cry today as we answer the call to serve Him. Over the many years that I have been involved in and committed to ministry serving the Lord, I have also "balked" at the commands (requests) that God has given to me in terms of "where I should be and what I should be doing."

My "balking" sometimes included questions such as, "Lord, why are You leading me to this place to serve You, and not that place? Are You sure that this is what You want me to do? I'm not so sure that I can handle this assignment on my own."

Sometimes when we are called and supposedly "committed" to serve the Lord, we often find ourselves (in the flesh) wanting or desiring to serve Him again from the perspective that our names might be emblazoned in bright lights on the marquee of the church or might become synonymous with the name of that church or ministry (Dr. Anthony J. Wiggins Ministries, for example).

There have always been some things or some areas of ministry that I would like to pursue and achieve for my own self-gratification and fulfillment, but ultimately, I have resigned myself to listen to the voice of the Lord for clear direction and to wait on Him to reveal to me exactly "what it is and where it is that He alone wants me to serve."

When you follow the voice of God and allow yourself to be attuned to His direction as well as to follow His will, you can never be wrong or led astray. True, people may never "know your name or appreciate or understand what you have done—or what you are doing." Remember that only what you do in serving the Lord and advancing His kingdom is going to be counted at the end.

Like so many that I know, and others that I perhaps will never know, I have always struggled with the belief that what I bring to the table, or what I have to offer, is not the best—or not even enough.

To that way of thinking, God constantly reminds me (2 Timothy 1:9), "He has not only called me but saved me with a holy calling that is not based on my works, but according to His own purpose that He has given to me in Jesus Christ sometime before He even created the foundations of the world."

Because of this promise, I have committed myself to trusting God alone completely with my life, knowing that He will always have and provide for me that which is nothing but the best for me as He sees it through the filter of His divine lens.

"Though my beginnings seem to be and in fact have been small, God promises and declares that my future will be prosperous as long as I love and serve Him" (Job 8:7).

No, the promise or the guarantee of a "prosperous life" promised by God is not one in His eyes that is going to be measured or fulfilled by the "worldly standards" of material possessions, monetary success measured by accumulating a vast financial portfolio, or some degree of notoriety or fame.

However, I pray by the grace of God that I cling and hold fast to achieving and fulfilling the full essence as well as the reality of His promise throughout my life of service for Him alone. When I have done this to the best of my God-given talent and ability, then indeed will my humble beginnings be prosperous in the way God intended and designed.

CHAPTER TWO
"IT'S NOT GOING TO BE EASY"

"But as for you, be strong and courageous, for your work shall be rewarded."
(2nd Chronicles 15:7, NLT)

One of the biggest misconceptions as well as misunderstandings that we as Christians have about the Christian life is that because we have chosen to live our lives following Jesus Christ, things are going to be easy. According to John 16:33, quite the opposite perspective becomes "crystal clear" and is true.

Our Savior Jesus Christ Himself issues a promise to us in the form of a warning that is poignantly painful: "In the world, expect to face trouble, adversity, and difficulty, but be encouraged that because I have overcome these challenges, you also can overcome."

No, God never promised us that the life we have chosen following Him was going to be easy, but He did promise that if we remain strong and courageous (2nd Chronicles 15:7) and fight the good fight of faith with all perseverance, He would be with us and reward us for our efforts!

As a child of God, I have found that in Jesus Christ there is certainly a sense of peace, contentment, prosperity, and joy, but also, we need to understand that there are and will be seasons and times of discouragement, disappointment, difficulty, and pain. Following Jesus is a lifelong journey that begins with a person first denying himself (or herself), "taking up their own individual cross," and following the path as well as the course that He has outlined for us to follow (Matthew 16:24).

There certainly are no shortcuts, and the cross that we have been called to bear is not and won't be easy. The "blessed assurance" that we have, however, is that our Lord Himself will be there with us when that cross becomes too heavy for us to bear alone (Luke 14:27; Psalm 55:22). Because of the goodness of God, His love, His grace, and His mercy, you will come to discover that we are never left to bear our burdens alone!

His grace has and always will be sufficient for us in the times of our weakest moments and our most difficult challenges. Recently (in August of 2024), my daughter Nichole and her husband Amir celebrated ten years of being married. Their words to me and my wife, Valerie, were: "Thanks, Mom and Dad, for setting the groundwork and modeling in front of us the example of what a successful marriage should look like. No, it hasn't been easy, but the result of what we are presently experiencing has been a blessing that only God can provide."

My prayer for them and all other young Christian couples as they continue to live their lives is that they continue to trust God and keep their faith in Him. "Anything worth having is certainly worth fighting for."

My journey, as well as my struggle, in accomplishing academic success and excellence (Today I hold a doctorate degree in practical theology), has been long and tedious. Upon graduating from high school (Shaw High School, East Cleveland, Ohio, retired an instructor), I remember being told and advised by my high school guidance counselor that "you don't possess the aptitude or the capability of attending college, so you should pursue a future working with your hands instead of your brain. Find a good-paying manual labor job and pursue that if you want to be successful."

After this initial assessment of my future with "those who were supposed to offer me hope and inspiration for my future," I came home dejected and shared with my father that "at school they said that I wasn't college material," and I concluded that "I guess I won't be going to college."

My father's response to me in January of 1970 still resonates in my heart and mind today, and still ignites a fire as well as a desire to excel and to achieve: He said, "Tony, never let anyone tell you what you can accomplish or achieve if that is what you want to do. If you want to go to college, then go!" I did, and as they say—the rest is history!

No, it has not been easy, and I am the first to admit it. By the grace of God, my work has been rewarded. Presently, I am an educator at Cleveland Central Catholic High School in Cleveland, Ohio, an instructor of Bible courses at Maranatha Bible College and Seminary in Cleveland, Ohio, and serve as the Senior Pastor of Friends Fellowship Bible Church also in Cleveland, Ohio! For the past eight years, I have also served as a hospice chaplain (pastor) for Adoration Hospice (also in Cleveland, Ohio).

Presently, I am in the process of writing this (my fifth book!)

Accomplishing these "milestones" in my life has come at the expense of sacrificing a great amount of time and commitment to being open to following what I believe to be and is the calling of God on my life. In and of myself, I know that it is the power of God alone that has allowed me to write these books, which I believe will be the source of encouragement to many others who one day might read what I have written.

Invariably, I am asked, "How is it that at your age (73 years old) you are still able to function at such a high level of energy in doing all of the things that you are presently doing?" (teaching, pastoring, serving as a hospice chaplain, and writing books). In part, my answer is the standard "God is good," but also, I am energized by the words of the prophet Nehemiah found in Nehemiah 8:10: "The joy of the Lord indeed is my strength!" And I find myself not only continuously strengthened but also energized by His power with the amazing capacity as well as the ability to meet the challenges of life head-on with the mindset and the determination that just won't allow me to stop what I am doing.

I stand in awe and am still amazed when I recall sitting in the presence of my late uncle (Rev. Dr. Ezell Wiggins) as he preached before a crowd of believers at church a few years ago at the age of 90, shortly before going home to be with the Lord!

Zechariah 4:6 further encourages me that whatever I do, "it is not by might, nor is it by power, but it is by my spirit, saith the Lord of hosts." Recently, my own beloved and esteemed pastor (Rev. Dr. Eddie L. Hawkins) gave his last sermon about three weeks ago before his church, which he had pastored for 50 years. He was 89 years old, and on the cusp of being 90, two weeks before he died in September of 2024!

I now understand the passion and the desire to serve the Lord that these two men certainly had as they sacrificed and committed their lives to serving the Lord with gladness. Sure, it was hard, and nothing deterred them—not even sickness and failing health that both encountered in their later days as they preached the Word of God "in and out of the seasons" of their lives.

Nowhere in scripture have I found yet where God assures me that because I have Him present in my life, indwelling me through His Holy Spirit, that things for me or for any other believer are going to be easy. On the contrary, His "promise" to me (John 16:33) offers the stark reality that "In the world we are going to have difficulties, problems, frustrations, and pain—but to remain composed and confident that we shall overcome because our Lord Himself has already overcome."

Paul and Silas were just two of the many biblical characters who, though they suffered and endured hard and difficult times because they chose to serve the Lord through proclaiming His Word, were throughout these times still able to offer heartfelt praise, worship, and thanks to God for sustaining them. Acts 16 recounts that one day, as these two men of God were going down to embark on a time of prayer, they were met by a young girl who was possessed by demons. (She had a spirit of divination.)

Her "masters" profited greatly from her ability to "tell the fortunes of others." However, this young woman decided to align herself with Paul and Silas and made it known to others that these two men were servants of the Most High God and were declaring words of deliverance and salvation. After listening to this young demon-possessed girl give what Paul took to be a demonic approval of his preaching, Paul cast the demon out of this girl under the authority of the name of Jesus Christ (Acts 16:18).

This girl's master became distraught about what Paul had done because now their "instrument for financial gain" (the power of the demon-possessed girl to tell fortunes for profit) was lost to them. They proceeded to bring charges against the teachings of Paul and Silas to the authorities (magistrates) for teaching customs and beliefs that Roman citizens did not adhere to, and had both Paul and Silas arrested, beaten, and thrown into prison (Acts 16:19–24).

Again, it's not always going to be pleasant or easy when you decide to serve the Lord in spreading the good news of the Gospel, but we can remain confident that God will never close His eyes or His ears to the service that we provide in His name. At midnight in prison, Paul and Silas conducted a prayer meeting and worship and praise service to God despite their incarceration!

True to His Word and His promise, God sent an earthquake that loosened the very foundations of the prison walls, Paul and Silas' shackled chains were broken, and even those who were commissioned to ensure that these two men of God were to remain confined to their prison cells cried out themselves and were saved! (Acts 16:25–31)

Not only was the Philippian jailor (the one responsible for securing Paul and Silas' incarceration) converted, but he later became a helpful assistant to these two men of God, and his entire family acknowledged and received salvation (Acts 16:32–34). No matter how difficult the challenge and the calling placed upon us to serve the Lord might be, the result of the "fruit of our labor" is all that ultimately is going to matter when we stand before the presence of God one day!

Personally, I am learning more each day as I continue my walk of faith and service to the Lord not to "whine and complain" about why God placed me in such a position that I am in where there seems to be no way out, and no one (other than God Himself) seems even to care whether I succeed or not, or whether I am "productive."

For some twenty-five years, the only "church home" and ministry that I have ever really known was the Good Shepherd Baptist Church in Cleveland, Ohio, under the pastorate and leadership of our beloved esteemed pastor, the late Dr. Eddie L. Hawkins, who recently went home to be with the Lord in

September of 2024—ironically while I am writing this book. My family joined this "little house church" when I was ten years old! (in 1962).

It was here in this modest little flourishing church that my faith in God and love for His work was nurtured and developed into what now has become an over forty-year commitment of following God, serving in ministry of some form from ushering and singing in the choir as a child, to teaching Sunday School, serving on the Deacon Board, and ultimately preaching the Word of God, and pastoring a church!

After 25 years of being instructed, taught, and eventually officially "ordained" to preach the Gospel of Jesus Christ in 1985 by my now late pastor Dr. Eddie L. Hawkins, (Good Shepherd Baptist Church), God "called" me to my "first" pastoral ministry in January of 1988, when I was selected and appointed as the Assistant Pastor of the Bright Star Missionary Baptist Church by the founding and present pastor, Dr. David Hunter (now retired). I "left the comfy, cushy confines of my beloved home church" (Good Shepherd Baptist Church), whose membership was at that time just under 800 members, to serve with Pastor David Hunter at Bright Star, to serve with a "smaller yet flourishing and promising church of just about 250 members."

Many of my friends were baffled and confused as to why I would leave a larger and more prestigious position of ministry to serve God in a "smaller place," but I knew, understood, and trusted God's call on my life by enlarging my territory and allowing me to serve Him in a position of pastoral leadership, which I did for some twenty years with Pastor David Hunter at the Bright Star Missionary Baptist Church as the Assistant Pastor. Again, this work wasn't easy, but it was a wonderful, beautiful, and challenging time of growing, developing, and propelling me into the man of God and the Christian leader that I am today—and I thank God for this amazing time of stepping out on faith to enhance my relationship of faith further and trust in Jesus Christ!

It was in this time of serving the Lord under the pastorate of Dr. David Hunter and learning all of the nuances of pastoral ministry firsthand, that I can truly say that God allowed me to foster and to develop a heart and a mind for preparing myself to the best of my ability to ensure that the total needs of the "church" (the body of committed believers and followers of Jesus Christ) are being met according to the standards and the principles of the Word of God. Without a heart and a mind for the things of God as well as a heart and a mind for the people of God, we as leaders have failed in our call to serve God, and our efforts and all of our labor at best are in vain.

In Matthew chapter 28, verses 19 and 20, particularly, we (believers and followers of God through and because of Jesus Christ) received a very clear but simple directive for our call to action: "Go ye therefore into all the world, teach, preach, and make disciples of all nations." Wherever God calls us to go to minister for Him, we should commit ourselves to answering that call, even if we are called to labor and to toil in positions that are not on the "radar screen" of ever having even the most remote opportunity or chance of us gaining the applause and the accolades of men and women for our efforts.

After all, all that we do in spreading the gospel of Jesus Christ is that His name alone might be uplifted and receive all the glory, the honor, and the praise. John the Baptist, the voice of one crying out in the wilderness to "make way for the coming of the Lord," said it best in the gospel of St. John chapter 3 and verse 30: "He (Jesus Christ) must increase, and I must decrease"—simply meaning that the most important task that has been set before us is that of simply being an "instrument" available to share and to spread the good news of the gospel of Jesus Christ and His coming kingdom, and not that of trying to promote ourselves over and above God's plan for us.

It all starts and ends with us being able to humble ourselves and seek the agenda of Jesus Christ, because in His own way and in His own time, He will elevate us to higher positions for His glory.

In January of 2006, God called me from a "comfortable" position in a church (Bright Star Missionary Baptist Church, Cleveland, Ohio) where I had been serving as the assistant pastor to the senior pastor for some eighteen years. I have come to the realization as well as the understanding that when God "calls" us to serve Him in whatever position of ministry in whatever part of the country or the world that He calls us to serve Him, I'll never forget His (God's) definitive message to me: "I want you to go out from the place that you are presently serving, and begin a brand-new ministry, a church that will serve an entirely different type of people as the focus of its ministry." The rest, as they say, "is history," and on January 1st, 2006, along with the help and support of 12 friends, God led me to "birth" our new ministry, "The Friends Fellowship Bible Church" in my home in East Cleveland, Ohio—home of my wife, Valerie, and me (13900 Potomac Avenue). We literally turned the living room and dining room of our home into a place of worship and praising the Lord each Sunday morning!

This modest and simple beginning of our church continued to hold services in our home until Easter of 2006, when we were privileged and blessed to relocate our church to the "Korb Lounge" of the old Shaw High School, just about three or four minutes from our home.

As I look back over the humble and modest beginnings of this phase of my ministry, I can certainly say that it has not, by any stretch of the imagination, been an easy undertaking. But because God is and always has been faithful and true to His Word, our ministry was able to flourish and succeed in what I now see from the perspective of what I call a "non-traditional church."

For just about a seven-year time in the ministry of the church that I still proudly serve today as the founding and Senior Pastor (Friends Fellowship Bible Church, in Cleveland, Ohio), I had the unique privilege as well as the opportunity to serve as the executive director of a halfway house residential facility (ARCA, Accepting Responsibility, Changing Attitudes). This organization was responsible for helping to meet the demanding physical, emotional, and employment needs of a group of 'marginalized' young and middle-aged adults facing the overwhelming challenge of trying to reacclimate themselves into a world and a society that they had difficulty fitting into because of a series of problems ranging from drug addiction to homelessness.

One day, a very good friend and member of our church (Cherisse), who also happened to serve as our financial secretary, in addition to serving as the Human Resource Director at ARCA, approached me about possibly serving as a board member of this organization. I readily accepted this opportunity, and by the hand of God, it wasn't too long before I was asked to serve as ARCA's

Executive Director! In time, most of (if not all) the twenty or more men and women housed in our residential facility began to attend Sunday morning worship services at our church, and again, because of God's direction, this "marginalized" group of men and women accepted Jesus Christ as their Lord and Savior—and their lives began to change!

I still look back at the time when we (our "non-traditional church") held baptism services for these new converts of faith in Jesus Christ! I was never left again wondering "when and how" our fledgling church, which started in the front living room in our home (my wife Valerie and I) was going to expand and grow physically!

No, it wasn't easy, but God has blessed us then, and even after going through the two years of COVID (2020–2022), when most public facilities and churches were forced to close, with some eventually during this time being totally wiped out and obliterated, we have been able to survive. God, through His mercy and grace, has allowed us as a church to weather the storm.

Prior to the relentless attack of COVID (2020–2022), our church was physically housed in a "warehouse building" complex that could easily accommodate up to three hundred people for our weekly Sunday morning worship services. Our "space" included six nicely-sized classrooms, an office/study for me (the pastor), and a nice kitchen area capable of providing hot meals whenever we needed time and space for our social functions and other celebratory gatherings.

Unfortunately, during the two-year COVID period, like a vast majority of public places like churches and restaurants, we were not allowed to meet for Sunday morning worship services, but were committed and "forced" to pay our monthly $2,000 bill for leasing our worship space. Like so many other churches, once COVID "ran its course," we were able to resume our worship services once a month, only to discover that more than half of our church members chose only to participate and attend church services online.

Again, by the grace of God, we were able to downsize our worship space to half its original size at half of the cost, and are still today, like so many other churches, trying to regroup and reclaim our pre-COVID standard of Sunday morning worship and ministry experiences. No, it hasn't been easy, but as a church, we are still open, regrouping, moving forward, and trusting God to help us rebuild our church in this time of post-COVID fallout. The calling, the command, and the need to get the message of Salvation out to a lost and dying world remain the same, and will never change, despite the difficult times that will always continue to challenge us.

In no way am I attempting to compare the early church's persecution, as recounted in the book of Acts chapter 8, to what many churches experienced during the two-year COVID dilemma, but there are some things in common for us to consider, and some lessons that we can learn from it.

During the time of the church's persecution, again, as it is outlined in Acts Chapter 8, we can see the church ultimately experience a time of physical growth and, in what I also believe was a time of spiritual growth, during a widespread time of persecution.

During this time of great persecution that resulted in many Christian leaders being arrested and thrown into prison for simply preaching the message of Salvation through Jesus Christ, and some like Stephen even losing their lives, the church was able to prosper, to thrive, and to grow. Regardless of the magnitude or the difficulty of the times and the uncertainty of the dilemmas that we have faced, God remains forever faithful to us, just as He has promised that He would.

I still find encouragement from what I personally perceive as one of God's most iconic promises found in the book of Isaiah 54:17: "No weapon that is formed against thee shall prosper, and every tongue that shall rise against thee in judgment thou shalt condemn. This is the heritage of the Lord, and their righteousness is of me, saith the Lord."

This powerful promise is a blessing from God, assuring us (me and you), His people, of protection as well as vindication from every situation, occurrence, and form or shape of opposition that would even think or dare to "rise up" or even speak against us to cause us any evil or wicked misfortune. God's power will ultimately destroy them along with their subversive plans for our demise.

No, it definitely hasn't been easy, and neither is it going to be easy as we move forward in our calling by God to, as the "Great Commission" calls and challenges us in the Gospel of Matthew chapter 28, go forth into all of the world and spread the good news of Jesus Christ by sharing the message of hope, salvation, and redemption for a lost and dying world—that it is only your faith and trust in God and accepting Him as your Lord and Savior that will be the only way to be secured and sustained in a world that has little or no hope in peace, contentment, and survival apart from embracing and endorsing this ultimate message of faith.

Ironically, at the time of my writing this book, the election for the next President of the United States of America had just concluded. I'm not going to go into a discourse or a debate about which candidate you supported to become the 47th President of the United States (Kamala Harris or Donald Trump) because I know for a fact that God Himself is neither Democrat nor Republican!

Regardless of the fact that Donald Trump is poised to become the next President of the United States as a result of one of the most significantly important elections of my lifetime, it's not going to be easy, given the times and the conditions of our world's chaotic climate and affairs.

As my eleventh and twelfth-grade high school students entered my Theology classroom at Cleveland Central Catholic High School the day after the November election of 2024, many were distraught and visibly shaken by the news that, despite their hopes and prayers for a different outcome, Donald Trump was now the President-Elect of the United States of America, with the inauguration set for January of 2025.

"Mr. Wiggins," one student asked me, "why did God allow Donald Trump to become President, and not Kamala Harris?" I thought for the eternity of a few seconds before responding, "You know, what's most important is the fact that whether Donald Trump or Kamala Harris becomes the next President of our country, the prospects and the hopes for your future as well as for mine—and even the entire world—have been and always will be in the hands of God, and determined by Him alone."

"Neither Kamala Harris nor Donald Trump has the power or the ability within themselves to determine what is going to happen and what our future is going to look like or eventually become—it is best to keep your faith and your trust in God because He is in control, and He never makes any mistakes."

"No, it's not going to be easy, but as for you and me, let us continue to pray, to trust in God, be strong and courageous (2nd Chronicles 15:7), and know that He (God) has each of us and the entire world in His hands. We are going to be alright. God has promised us, and He is a "man" who cannot lie." (Numbers 23:19). The best is yet to come.

Through the power of the faith that we have in God through Jesus Christ, God is able to transform our lives into just what it is that He wants us to become, and at the same time, provide us with much-needed guidance and direction as we face a world of uncertainties every day.

I can remember a time in the early years of my now forty-eight-year marriage, when we (my family) were struggling financially because I didn't have a job. By faith, I trusted and believed in God that, according to one of the "simple promises" of His Word (Philippians 4:19): "But my God shall supply all of your needs according to His riches in glory through Christ Jesus," He was going to fulfill this pressing need.

My unemployment had extended for about a two-to-three-month period, and our bills were beginning to get out of control. My wife (Valerie) and I had prayed together about this situation, and that Monday morning, I went out to "follow up" on a lead that I had for a teaching position at Saint Adalbert Catholic School (Cleveland, Ohio).

I remember telling my wife boldly and confidently that "I was not coming home without a job." To me, this statement echoed and reiterated my faith in God that He was going to open a door of opportunity for "right now today"! I was convinced of the fact that God knew my situation and that He was going to provide me with what I needed because He promised me that He would, according to His Word.

During my interview with the principal of the school (Mrs. Lydia Harris), she informed me that there were some forty-odd candidates under consideration for two open teaching positions, and that she would, over the course of the next two weeks, be making final decisions as school was scheduled to begin in about two months. With this information, I thought, "Wow, my chances for securing this position are just about 'nothing, but God.'"

For some unexplained reason (which I have always believed to be the hand of God's power at work intervening on my behalf), our conversation centered upon my knowledge of the St. Adalbert School and the St. Adalbert Church, of which the school was a part. I shared with Mrs. Harris that for several years, members of my family on my wife's side had been educated at The St. Adalbert School Parish and were still active members of the St. Adalbert Church.

Finally, upon my sharing with Mrs. Harris that Jordan and Joyce Sanders (my late uncle and aunt), along with Aunt Joyce's sister, "Sister Juanita Shealey," a very well-known and revered member of the city of Cleveland, Ohio's Catholic Diocese were "a part of my family," she extended one of the two open teaching positions available at the school to me ***on the spot!***

She went on to say, "I consider your Aunt Joyce and your Uncle Jordan, and of course the highly esteemed Sister Juanita, as part of my family, and if you are a part of their family, one of these two open teaching positions is yours!" What an amazing blessing from God, and the next twelve years of my life were spent as an educator at St. Adalbert Catholic School, teaching fifth to eighth graders! In the midst of our greatest challenges, God always proves Himself to be concerned about not only hearing, but also answering our prayers.

Once again, I realized, understood, and appreciated the faithfulness of God, who always has been and forever will be true to His promise to provide me, one of His children, with that which I needed! (Philippians 4:19) By the grace of God, this was the "official beginning" of my career as an educator in 1987, even extending until now in 2024!

No, it hasn't been easy, but God has rewarded me for my faith in Him, and the best is still yet to come as I look to Him and lean upon Him for directing my life and helping me to understand that in His appointed time, it will make sense.

CHAPTER THREE
"THE POWER OF FAITH"

"For everyone born of God overcomes the world. This is the victory that has overcome the world, even our faith."
(1st John 5:4, NIV)

Rest assured, and believe that there is no power anywhere in this world that can compare to the power of the faith that you and I have or should have in God. The Power of Faith (Biblical Faith) is a powerful concept that helps us as Christians to form and maintain our personal relationship with God. Through this faith, we have the unique experience of accessing God's love, His guidance, as well as His never-ending presence in our lives.

Furthermore, this faith in God also allows us to forge our ability to grow in wisdom as well as the knowledge of understanding God, which in turn leads to our spiritual maturity. We should continuously be in the habit of thanking and praising God that through this faith, we are empowered with the fortitude and the capacity to address the many challenges as well as the obstacles that arise in our lives daily.

We can rely upon the strength of God and all that He provides for us rather than relying upon our own feeble, limited resources found within our own strength. This faith in God alone has the power not only to change our lives, but also it has the power to provide us with a sense of unparalleled hope needed for our future.

According to God's Word, this is the faith that we are called and commanded to "walk by" each day of our lives instead of trusting in what we can see with our own eyes and imagine in our own minds. It is the answer of all things that we place the premise of our "hope" in God (2nd Corinthians 5:7; Hebrews 11:1).

Without this faith, we can never expect to please God or to accomplish that which He has decreed and set before us during our lives of service to Him. Hebrews (11:6) further assures me that it has been this faith alone that has kept me, blessed me, and allowed me to keep moving along the path of life that God has called me to—which has included hills and valleys, as well as twists and turns of every sort along the way.

It is this power of faith, regardless of how great or how small it is, that touches the heart of God, ensuring us that not only does He see our needs but also that He answers our prayers according to the need to allow His work to be done in our lives. According to Matthew 17:20–21, Jesus himself tells us that "if we have faith the size of a 'mustard seed,' mountains can be moved from blocking the path of our lives, and that nothing will be impossible for us to achieve or to accomplish."

I don't know about you, but there have been countless times in my life that my faith has been tested, only to prove that God is who He says He is and is more than capable of doing all that He promised He would do for me because of the relationship that I have with Him through Jesus Christ.

As the famous songwriter Lidie H. Edmunds (Eliza E. Hewitt) wrote in her testimonial, soul-touching hymn in 1891, "My soul indeed has found a resting place," and that place is firmly and securely entrenched in Jesus Christ. Because of this faith, you and I can overcome all of the challenges of life that are going to come our way. This hymn goes on to say, "It is enough that Jesus died, but more importantly, that He died for me." This has been and continues to make all the difference in my life as I go on trusting Him every step of the way!

As parents raising children, we should value and treasure each moment that we spend with them because life passes much too quickly. I thank and praise God that I was raised in a strong Christian home by parents and a host of grandparents, uncles, and aunts who "poured" out of themselves and "modeled" all the faith and the trust in God that was shared and instilled in them, into me.

This faith in God has been and continues to be the foundation of how I have built and lived my life in regard to everything that I think, that I do, and that which I say.

In 1998, my wife and I became "empty nesters" as our daughter Nichole and our son Michael both graduated from high school (Shaw High School in East Cleveland, Ohio). We were very proud of the fact that our children were now alumni of the same school that both my wife, Valerie, and I had attended.

Michael was the first to leave home as he "shipped" out to complete basic training with the United States Army just about one week after graduation, and Nichole left for college in August (1998). We hoped and prayed all their young lives that the faith, trust, and confidence that we have in God had been poured into their lives and instilled into their hearts as they set out to make their mark on the world.

Faith in God means little until tested. Time would soon reveal whether our children, now on the brink of adulthood, were ready to live on their own—carried by the prayers their mother and I had whispered over them all their lives.

As parents, we never relish the idea that one day we would have to "cut the umbilical cord" that connected us to our children, but it had to be done, as painful as it was and seemed to be.

Our daughter Nichole was only a short 60 miles away from home, attending my Alma Mater, Ashland University, in Ashland, Ohio. On the other hand, our son Michael was first sent to Fort Leonard Wood for basic training just outside of St. Louis, Missouri. This was just the first of many stops that young men and women like my son enlisting in the armed forces, serving our country, must make in fulfilling their military service.

Eventually, my son Michael's foray into the United States Army saw him spend time stationed in Texas, Alabama, and Georgia (to name a few stateside) and remote, faraway places around the world like Kuwait and Iraq.

Every step of my son's journey into his military career was taking him further and further away from us as a family. We learned to cherish every phone call that he made to us, as well as every letter that he wrote to us that would update his situation.

My wife and I did our best to raise Michael and Nichole in a strong Christian home where we not only stressed the significance and the importance of having a personal relationship with Jesus Christ, but we also put forth our best effort to model that lifestyle in front of them daily.

Having a pastor for a father didn't automatically ensure that the power of the faith that I had (and still have in God) would simply just "pass over" and transfer to my children and become that essential part of their life upon which they could eventually build a solid Christian lifestyle.

From the time that my children were very young (especially from the time when they were between the ages of 2 and 6 years old), I would spend time every night reading to them from the Bible and sharing short stories about various individuals from it and how their faith in God kept and sustained them throughout the course of their lives. In 2006, shortly before my son deployed to Iraq, I had the chance to spend time with him—what would, ironically, be the last time before his death in the war in 2007. It became "crystal clear" to me then that my son indeed fully recognized and embraced his relationship with Jesus Christ and that he did have his own "power of faith."

My last conversation with Michael included me expressing some concern about his welfare as well as his safety on the battlefields of Iraq. As I hugged and embraced my son for the last time, he whispered his last words to me in my ear, which set my soul at ease and at peace, underscoring the power of faith that he now, as a young man, had in God. He simply said: "Don't worry, Dad, God will take care of me."

Above all else, God has proven Himself to be faithful to me, and all that I had to do was to exhibit that faith in Him, "the size of a mustard seed," and allow Him to complete His work of faith in my life. As a result, I have been able to experience and see the hand of God working in my life, even when there have been times that cause me to cry, and I don't even understand why difficulty and hard and difficult times have found their way into my life.

On January 23, 2007, my only son, Staff Sergeant Michael J. Wiggins, lost his life in the Iraq War. And it has been nothing but the power of the faith that my family and I have in God that has been able to sustain us and give us peace despite the hurt and the pain of this great personal loss. The passage of scripture in the Word of God recorded in Isaiah 26:3 continues to bring comfort and reassurance to our souls: God has promised us—me and each of you reading this book—"that He will keep us in perfect peace as long as our hearts and our minds are stayed on Him."

I have come to the point in my life that, regardless of the situations and the circumstances that I have encountered and will continue to encounter until God calls me home or Jesus returns, I am determined to walk by faith, not by sight, and to trust in the power of God's never-ending love for me and the faith that I have in Him.

Recently, just a few days before Christmas of this year (2024), a dear friend of more than 25 years and an esteemed and devoted educator, as well as a co-worker of mine (at Cleveland Central Catholic High School in Cleveland, Ohio) (Joe Rock), lost his mother in a tragic automobile accident just a few moments after attending a Christmas program for her granddaughter. (Joe's five-year-old daughter, Maria).

In one of our conversations just a few days after this tragic, life-shattering event, Joe shared with me some painful details of what happened on that December 16, 2024, night: "Rev. Tony" (one of the names he often called me) he said, "we just left from Maria's program and as we were walking back to our cars, I asked my mom if she needed me to walk her to her car. She said, 'I got it. I'll see you later.' My response, which is what I always have told my mom every day after talking with her in person or on the phone, was, 'I love you, Mom.'

"Seemingly, a split second after turning to walk back to my car, we heard a car turn the corner, swerving out of control, with screeching tires, and literally running over someone. In that same instance, the driver of the car took off!

My gut feeling told me that it was my mom, and as I turned around, I saw her (my mom) lying in the street. My daughter Maria was crying, I was screaming and yelling as I grabbed and hugged Maria, and my wife was by my mom's side holding her hand. It all seemed to be surreal as it unfolded in front of me in slow motion."

Joe's next words and statement posed to me as a question that gripped my heart as he said, "Pastor Tony, it was only a matter of eight steps or so that my mother had to walk across the parking lot to return to her car. Why did God turn His back on my mom for those last steps of her life and allow this to happen? My faith has taken a big hit, and I don't know if and when I will ever recover."

"Joe," I said, "I know the depth of your pain. It's going to take time."

In the 25 or so years that I have known Joe and his mother, I personally can attest to the power of the faith that Joe's mom had in God and that she and Joe's dad had poured into his life. Not only is Joe a man of faith, but also a man of great integrity.

Over the course of our relationship, Joe is one of the very few people that I have shared intimate, personal facts and details about my life with. We've shared many conversations about just about everything from interracial marriage to teaching kids in school for over 25 years, to the deaths of my brother and sister, my mom and dad, my son Michael's death in Iraq, the loss of Joe's dad, and now to the loss of his mother.

Considering this tragic loss of his mom just a few days before Christmas, Joe further questioned me. "Pastor Tony, I don't know how you, your wife, and Nichole (our daughter) have been able to survive mentally, spiritually, and even physically in the midst of all that you have lost, especially your son Michael's death."

"Personally, I am having the most difficult time of my life. There were some days that I thought I would lose my mind. My heart has literally been ripped out of my chest!"

"Does the pain ever go away? Do the tears ever stop flowing? Does God even care?"

Both my wife and I were at a loss for words. We pondered carefully for a few seconds, which seemed like an eternity, before responding: "Joe, there is nothing wrong with questioning God when things like what you and I have experienced happen, and one of the toughest lessons to learn is that He (God) never makes mistakes.

"God has designed it so that every time you shed tears, it will help you to bring closure to what you have experienced and will help you become stronger in making the needed adjustment to a life that you will have to live without your mother's physical presence."

"My wife and I still shed tears today, even as we approach nineteen years since Michael's death, but yet because of the power of the faith that we have in God, His promise to never leave us, along with His love, grace, and mercy, we have been able to move on with our lives. It will take time, but the tears will stop flowing, the sun will shine again, and laughter will be restored to your life, just as God has promised."

"Draw closer to God, and He will draw closer to you."

"No, it hasn't been easy, and it won't be, but we have emerged from our tragic loss not bitter, but better, tempered by the hand of God touching our lives in ways that we could never experience without suffering what we have lost. God promises us that He will be drawn closer to the broken-hearted and will become for us much more than we have lost."

The power of faith in God, if we understand it and allow it to manifest itself in our lives, has the power to transform the very way we think, act, and live our lives positively as we transition through life and all its challenges and changes. I have found that in all things that I have experienced and yet one day will experience, God's grace is sufficient.

The nineteenth-century German philosopher Friedrich Nietzsche is credited with coining the popular aphorism "That which doesn't kill you will make you stronger." As a Christian and a devout reader of God's Word, I have discovered and believe that Nietzsche "borrowed" this famous quote from Jeremiah 12:5 and 2nd Corinthians 12:9, (if you have run a race with men on foot and have been worn out, how can you win a race against horses?)

Your resiliency must have some support, which I attribute to be the faith that I (we) have in the power of God to not quit or to give up despite the toughest of times. Going a bit further in the Bible, 2nd Corinthians 12:9 tells us that it is in the midst of our weakest moments and experiences that God's strength takes up and finds root in our lives, making us stronger with the ability to withstand and endure difficulty.

For my friend Joe Rock and so many others who might one day read this book, let me offer some words of encouragement. "As long as you have and maintain the power of faith that you have in God, along with hope and a willingness to trust in Him in the midst of your greatest challenges and trials, it can and will lead you to a sense of spiritual renewal that will enhance your life in addition to offering a sense of comfort and peace not just for your own benefit, but as a blessing to someone else who one day unfortunately, experiences that which you have experienced."

"I believe that what defines and describes a person's life is not what he/she goes through in life, but rather how they emerge from that which they have gone through… God alone knows the plan that He has for our lives, and none of those plans are meant to hurt us but to serve as a means of allowing us to "prosper" and to give us hope and a future. (Jeremiah 29:11). With God in our lives, the best is yet to come…"

Chapter Four
"Perseverance:
A Willingness to Never Quit"

"Let us not become weary in doing good, for at the proper time we will reap a harvest if we don't give up."
(Galatians 6:9, NIV)

Biblically, perseverance can be defined as an act of "faithful endurance." This virtue of our Christian faith is a call or a command from God to us as believers, committed by faith in Him, to withstand hard times of suffering with joy and the willingness to trust in God regardless of what we have experienced in life, as well as the prospects of what we have yet to experience in our lives in the days and the years to come.

Recently, I made a phone call to my daughter Nichole, but she didn't answer at the time. Her voicemail message for whoever called was one of encouragement: "Sorry, I can't take your call right now, but if life gives you a bowl of lemons, make some lemonade!" My response to her voicemail was: "I'll take two cups of lemonade to go!" An important message to learn here is that "your outlook determines your outcome." "If you think you can, then you will, but if you think that you can't, then you probably never will."

Our lives from the cradle to the grave can be seen as a "marathon race" that requires persistence and patience, as the writer of the book of Hebrews (many believe to be the Apostle Paul) encourages us in Hebrews 12:1: "Let us lay aside every sin and all of those things (weights) that so easily beset us and run with patience the race that is set before us—looking to or fixing our eyes on Jesus Christ, the author as well as the finisher of our faith."

When I was in high school (Shaw High School in East Cleveland, Ohio), I was a member of the track and field team. We dutifully committed ourselves to practice every day (Monday through Friday). On Thursday afternoons, we were engaged in competition with other schools in our league (The Lake Erie League Conference).

One of the star sprinters on our team (Leroy Burfitt), who is still a good friend of mine today and has been since we were in the fourth grade together, came up with a simple yet strategic plan that we followed in practice every day. As we trained and practiced each day, Leroy suggested that we wear three- to five-pound weighted vests under our track suits that would force us to exert more effort in our daily training routine.

On the day of our inter-school competitions, of course, we would take off the weighted vests, and it gave us the "illusion as well as the perception" that the race was easier than the training that we had undergone. It must have worked because I never saw my friend Leroy lose a race in two years, and he was always the league champion sprinter in both the 100- and 220-yard races! (In our day, we ran by yards and not by meters, which is today's standard!)

There is no other way that we are going to successfully run with the hope of finishing the race of our lives without the help of the hand of God—ordering our steps, directing our lives, and giving us the wisdom, the knowledge, and the perseverance to overcome life's challenges. (Perseverance, I believe, is what determines us.)

In this same passage of scripture, the writer (the Apostle Paul) further encourages us to run this race in the light of the "great cloud of witnesses" (Greek word Nephos), cheering us on, telling us that we can make it because they ran their race and overcame it. (This great cloud of witnesses mentioned in Hebrews 11 included Abel, Noah, Abraham, Isaac, Jacob, Sarah, and Moses, just to name a few—I believe that among these witnesses are my father, my mother, my uncles, and even my son Michael, as well as a number of other family members and friends!)

By and because of their faith in God, these "faithful witnesses" ran their race. Their lives bear a testimony encouraging me and you today that we also can run the race of our lives set before us victoriously—with perseverance and the will to always fight on! Despite all the challenges that rise up against me, I must develop the will to never quit—with God's help, I won't!

As Leroy and I and our entire track and field team practiced and prepared for the "race" of the week against our rival neighborhood schools, we were "weighted" down by three- to five-pound weighted vests. Still, on the day of our "competitive race," we laid aside those weights and were able to run with patience (effectively) the race that was set before us. Invariably, we usually won more races than we lost.

In our Christian lives, I believe that God calls and challenges us to have strategic plans that include trusting in Him and looking to Him for direction as we face the many "races" set before us while living our lives. I have found that this is the only way that we (Christians) are going to have the fortitude and the capacity to persevere in hopes of succeeding in the race of and for our lives.

1 Chronicles 16:11 encourages us that in all that we attempt to do, we should "seek the Lord's face and His strength continually," with the mindset that whatever we encounter as we live our lives, God will supply us with all the resources we need to fulfill what He would have us do—being successful witnesses for spreading the Gospel message to a lost and dying world of sinners.

In addition to teaching high school (Theology classes at Cleveland Central Catholic High School, and Maranatha Bible College and Institute in Cleveland, Ohio), I also, for the past seven years, have served Northeastern Ohio as a Hospice Chaplain for Adoration Hospice, and for the past twenty years have served as the founder and Senior Pastor of Friends Fellowship Bible Church. Quite a challenge and an undertaking for a man of my years, I am often told! (But God is able.)

Needless to say, I know that in order for me to meet and fulfill all that is required of me in each of these "assignments" so that the spreading and the sharing of God's redemptive message of hope and salvation might be completed successfully, it requires a commitment to perseverance!

At times, it is often easy to become overwhelmed and exhausted by the unique complexity and the demands of each job that I have been called to do. Still, it is my faith as well as my confidence in God's direction, power, and strength that allows me to prevail. (Philippians 4:13: I can do all things through Christ who gives me the strength and the ability.)

Early on in my late son Michael's athletic career as a "middle distance runner" (races from 800 meters to 2 miles in distance), I witnessed in him a true degree of tenacity and perseverance when it came to running. Mike had a strong penchant while running in that he never particularly liked any of his competitors to be in front of him once he had established and found his "groove" in the course of any given competitive race.

I fondly recall one race that Mike competed in when he was about 12 or 13 years old (The Jr. Olympics 800-meter finals). In this qualifying round, he had to finish in the top three of his assigned "heat" to advance to the finals. Coming off the last turn and entering the final 200 meters of this race, Mike was just about in fifth place.

We yelled out (family and supporting friends), "Come on Mike, let's go," and watched him assimilate into his "final finishing kick" that both willed and propelled him to the finish line, exerting every bit of energy that he could muster as he leaned and strained for the tape—catching the lead runner before physically blacking out at the finish line!

My wife, my daughter, and I all rushed to the track to assist him, as his coach said, "He always does that when he finishes his races because he never wants to lose! You can't teach willpower and perseverance! Boy, does he have it!" When Mike regained his senses and composure, we took him to the doctor's office for a precautionary check-up.

The doctor's assessment simply said, "Your son's physical make-up and disposition" (Mike was only 4'11" tall at the time and weighed about eighty-five pounds soaking wet, fully clothed) "should be supplemented by encouraging him to take some vitamins and Ensure, but other than that, he will be okay."

This tenacity and perseverance did serve Mike well in all his endeavors throughout his short life (twenty-six years)—in all that he undertook to do, up to and including his time spent serving in the United States Army before losing his life in the Iraq War in 2007. His faith in God never waned, as I will always remember his last words to me before he died: "Don't worry, Dad. God will take care of me."

As a Christian, I am a strong believer and proponent that perseverance, faith, confidence, and a willingness to trust in God can serve us well in our decision to follow Him throughout our lives. Whatever we do in thought, word, or deed should all be done with the intent that we are called to serve Him (God) with all that we have (1 Corinthians 10:31).

One day, God Himself is going to reward us not just for the way that we ran our race, but also for the way that we finished it. Above all else, this is the one main factor that continuously motivates, encourages, and drives me toward my goal, which is to please God in all that I do.

In 1 Corinthians 9:24–27, I am further challenged and encouraged: "All participants run a race, but only one is going to win a prize. Run your race with a purpose—not with meaningless effort or aim—anticipating and expecting to win because of your effort or perseverance. You have trained and committed yourself to this cause." (my own translation)

I love the story of Job's perseverance in the Bible. The account of his perseverance is an inspirational testimony of godly patience and a commitment to worship, serve, and trust God—even though he suffered the most difficult of circumstances, sufferings, and trials. In the book of Job, we find him introduced as a man of impeccable integrity—"upright and blameless" in his character—and a true worshipper and believer committed to serving and following God (Job chapter 1).

In Job 1:2–4, we also find that our "great adversary" (the Devil, Satan) is fully dedicated and committed to his job of wreaking havoc in the lives of anyone and everyone professing faith in God and a commitment to serve and honor Him (1 Peter 5:8). It is his "lifelong mission" (underscored by and with the permission of God to attack us—Job 1:8–12). As a believer, always remember to distinguish between two important concepts about our Christian faith: "It is the Devil who tempts us, while it is God our Savior who allows us to be tested." Be careful to consider that when we boast about being Christians, the Devil will tempt us, daring us to prove it, while God allows us to be tested (as trials of faith—1 Peter 5:12).

True to His Word, God will never lead us, His children and followers, into temptation (Matthew 6:13), but will always make the necessary provisions we need to counteract and defend against the enemy's relentless attacks. As we read the story of Job and apply it today to our own lives, "this testing of our faith" will ultimately lead to the development of what we need in life to overcome all weapons formed against us—perseverance.

By the grace of God, tempered with His love and mercy, if we as believers allow "perseverance to complete its work in us" (which is the maturity of our faith), then we will eventually come to the point where we are "lacking nothing" (James 1:2–4).

Unfortunately, we, as believers, sometimes find ourselves stuttering, sputtering, and even at times giving up or giving out because we fail to realize that this "race of our lives" is a marathon challenge. It requires much more than we are often willing to give in committing ourselves to a regimen of consistent, continual effort and dedication to God's plan for direction, correction, and instruction.

Someone once told me (I don't exactly remember who) a simple but **profound acronym** for the word **BIBLE**:

B–asic

I–nstruction

B–efore

L–eaving

E–arth!

If we allow the precepts, the guidelines, the principles, and the truths of the Bible—the unadulterated Word of God—to be "hidden in our hearts," as King David implores in Psalm 119:11, we can successfully overcome whatever we are confronted with throughout the challenges of our lives.

Just to encourage us a bit further, in Joshua 1:6–9, you will find the only mention of the key to success in life: "Meditate upon the truth of the law from the Word of God daily. Don't turn to the right or to the left from this law. Be strong and courageous in all that you strive to do, and your way will be prosperous as well as successful."

God will faithfully deliver to us what He promised if we commit ourselves to what He asks and requests of us. I am fully convinced of this fact because of my faith in Him.

The words from a simple song that I learned in my teenage years continue to be the principle or the thought about perseverance that dictates, guides, and motivates me in my life and all my endeavors as a Christian—even today:

"I have decided to follow Jesus,

I have decided to follow Jesus,

I have decided to follow Jesus,

No turning back, no turning back!

Though no one joins me, still I will follow,

Though no one joins me, still I will follow,

Though no one joins me, still I will follow,

No turning back, no turning back!"

A word of caution: Nowhere does it say that your way or your path in life will be an easy journey. But if you make the committed, dedicated effort to **persevere by faith**, God will honor and bless that which you strive and undertake to do for Him!

As a witness, I have. What about you?

CHAPTER FIVE
"ROADBLOCKS"

"And it will be said: Build up, build up, prepare the road! Remove the obstacles out of the way of my people."
(Isaiah 57:14, NIV)

Regardless of the path that each of us decides to take throughout this journey of our lives, I can guarantee you one thing for sure—there are inevitably going to be **roadblocks** along the way. Believe it! One of the many "promises" to us from the Word of God that we don't readily cherish or willingly accept affirms this fact: "Man is born unto trouble as sure as the sparks fly upward." (Job 5:7) Translation: "Life is not going to be easy!"

Roadblocks can best be defined or categorized as some type of barricade or obstacle that appears in your life—sometimes seemingly from out of nowhere—attempting to prevent you (yes, and me too) from accomplishing some predetermined objective that we highly value, or feel obligated and driven to complete. Sadly, these roadblocks are a fact of life that each of us must come to grips with and contend with.

The only good thing that can be said about roadblocks in our lives is that they are only "temporary obstructions" that hinder our rendezvous with progress and success. With God's help and a committed effort on our part, they can be conquered.

One of the first of many roadblocks that appeared in my life goes all the way back to the time of my last two years attending high school. It was during these two years that I, like many high school students, began to narrow down my plans about whether a college education was part of my future goals and ambitions.

I'll be the first to admit that the high school transcript of my grades indicated that I was not "one of the best students" of the 1970 graduating class of Shaw High School (in East Cleveland, Ohio), but I proceeded to make plans for college anyway. (I did, in fact, have a "C" average, which was nothing to brag about.)

The day I sat down with my Guidance Counselor to assist in charting out my future educational career and goals was one of a "rude awakening." My counselor (I remember her name, but I won't divulge it) said to me in no uncertain terms with words I still remember today: "I don't think that you have the aptitude or the ability to attend college or to ever graduate with a college degree. You should find a nice vocation (like working with your hands in a factory or some type of industrial labor) more suitable to your competency!"

For a brief moment, my future and the goal of becoming one of the first in my family to attend and graduate from college were dashed by the implied reality that, according to my Guidance Counselor's assessment (stated in a rude but nice way), I was academically inferior, not capable of even pursuing a college education. Sadly, I was just one of the few African American students in our school given the same assessment.

Dejected mentally and emotionally, I came home that day to inform my dad that I wouldn't be attending college as I had planned—and as he had hoped—because "they said I wasn't smart enough." My dad challenged me that day with words that, some fifty-five years later, still ignite and kindle a fighting spirit inside of me:

"Tony," he said, "never as long as you live, let anyone tell you that you are not capable of accomplishing what you set in your heart and in your mind to achieve! If you trust and believe in God, it is possible!"

I applied to and was accepted at Ashland College (now Ashland University) (on academic probation) in Ashland, Ohio. No, attending college in preparation for my future career wasn't easy, but the struggle and the fight have been worth the effort! Here I am now in 2025, completing the manuscripts on my third and fourth books, respectively!

Not bad for someone classified as "academically inferior" by a high school counselor! One of my favorite quotes in life is that "challenges, obstacles, and roadblocks in your life can do one of two things—they can make you bitter, or they can make you better! You choose!"

Along the way, I faced many other roadblocks and obstacles, but in the spring of 1974, after much hard work and perseverance, I proudly graduated with my Bachelor of Science degree in Education! The prophetic words from Jeremiah 29:11 were beginning to manifest in my life: "For I know the plans I have for you, declares the Lord. Plans to prosper you, not to harm you, but to give you a future filled with hope." Because God has promised, He will deliver on what He has decreed.

God always remains faithful to the promises of His Word that He declares over our lives, and more and more I am beginning to walk in the reality of this dynamic truth. For me, this was only the beginning, because finally, in 2005, by the grace of God, I proudly earned and received my Th.D. degree! (Doctor of Theology)

Roadblocks in our lives (thrown up by our enemies) will continue to attempt to impede our pathway to success, and the "naysayers" will continue to cause us to doubt whether accomplishing our desired goal is possible—but be encouraged, because our Lord and Savior Jesus Christ has promised us: "Because I have overcome, you shall also be able to overcome." (John 16:33)

Today, as an educator of high school students (now retired), I continue to challenge them in regard to their future dreams and aspirations: "If you look in a mirror, you will see a reflection of the only person capable of becoming a roadblock, a barricade, or an obstacle to you not becoming the successful person that God intends and calls for you to become. We are capable of doing all things through Christ, who gives us the strength." (Philippians 4:13)

In 1987, when I was an educator of seventh and eighth-grade students at St. Adalbert Catholic School in the "heart of the hood" in Cleveland, Ohio, I had the privilege of meeting a young man (Earl Boykins) whose story remains a fascinating account of one who overcame obstacles and barriers in life to accomplish one of his lifelong goals.

On the first day of class that year (1987), I traditionally asked each student to share with the class at least one thing they hoped to accomplish in life, even while growing up and attending school in the Fairfax Community of Hough in Cleveland, Ohio.

I always shared with my students the dubious distinction of the history of the community in which our proud school stood (and still stands today) as a beacon of hope and the fulfillment of dreams. I was so impressed by this school's academic excellence that while I was employed at St. Adalbert School as an educator, I enrolled my own two children as students.

For those unfamiliar with Cleveland, Ohio's history, during the summer of July 18th–23rd, 1966, the notorious Hough Riots unfolded just a short distance from our school. Racial tensions and unrest had been simmering in this now racially segregated community of Cleveland since the 1950s.

During the 1950s, there was a large exodus of middle-class white residents leaving this community, while middle-class African Americans moved in. Most of the businesses were still owned and operated by white proprietors, even though by 1966 the community was nearly 100% African American. Although Black residents of Hough comprised only 7% of Cleveland's population, 60% of reported crimes in the city occurred in Hough.

Schools and housing were inferior, as were the social services available to struggling residents. On a hot summer day—July 18, 1966—a white restaurant owner in Hough refused a Black patron a glass of water, triggering six days of social unrest: violence, looting, and the destruction of many businesses. (Much dispute still exists today over the true causes of these infamous, now-called "race riots," which occurred in many cities across our country.)

I personally remember, as a resident of Cleveland, when martial law was declared. Some 1,700 members of the National Guard were called in, and armored tanks rolled up and down the streets of Hough (accompanied by soldiers) to restore law and order. There were 275 arrests, and four Black residents were killed. Millions of dollars in property damage occurred, and some of those destroyed areas remain "undeveloped" in 2025—serving as a somber reminder of our city's violent past.

It is important to understand the relevance of our school (St. Adalbert) in the heart of this community. Largely, the students were unaware of just what their education would mean for their future. The neighborhood itself was, to some degree, a roadblock that each of the students attending this school had to overcome.

Again, on that first day of school in 1987, as he stood by my desk, I asked Earl Boykins what he aspired to achieve and accomplish in his lifetime. I'll never forget Earl's response that day:

"Mr. Wiggins," Earl said, "one day I am going to play professional basketball in the NBA!"

The amazing thing is that he (Earl) stood only about five feet tall, and later in life, he eventually grew to just about five feet, five inches! My initial thought—which I kept to myself—was, "Doesn't this kid know that professional basketball players are usually much taller and bigger than he'll ever grow to be?" That was going to be a major roadblock to his dream.

My response to Earl that day was the same response my dad had given me when I was in high school:

"Earl, never let anyone tell you what you can or cannot become—or do—if you devote and commit yourself to what it takes to accomplish your goal. Make sure that in pursuit of your dreams, you also earn your college degree."

Later, while attending Cleveland Central Catholic High School in Cleveland, Ohio, Earl led his school team to the Ohio State Basketball Championship (1993) and earned a college scholarship to Eastern Michigan University in 1994. After much hard work, dedication, and perseverance, Earl played professionally in the NBA for thirteen years!

In fact, throughout his NBA career, Earl played for ten teams, including the Denver Nuggets, Washington Wizards, Golden State Warriors, Charlotte Bobcats, and his hometown team, the Cleveland Cavaliers! At present, Earl is an assistant coach at UTEP (University of Texas at El Paso) and is doing a great job.

I am proud to say that I know this young man personally and that I had the opportunity of being one of his teachers in seventh and eighth grade. I proudly witnessed him overcoming tremendous odds, obstacles, and roadblocks to accomplish his dreams.

To me, Earl remains a "living testimony" that roadblocks in our lives only exist if we allow them to control and dominate us. He truly exemplifies one of my favorite passages of Scripture found in Philippians 4:13:

"I can do all things through Christ who gives me the strength."

Throughout the course of our lives, we all (whether we profess to be Christians or not) are going to encounter many obstacles, challenges, and roadblocks that will test our resolve. The Bible is literally filled with the amazing stories of characters who faced immense challenges and hardships during their lives.

It was only through their faith in God, coupled with perseverance, that they were able to overcome these struggles and the roadblocks that these struggles caused them to have in pursuit of their aspirations, goals, and dreams.

At some point in our lives, we as believers must realize and understand that it is our faith in God alone that is the impetus propelling us forward with the idea and the mindset that we can not only contend with but overcome whatever it is that tries to block our paths.

Without detailing their own unique individual stories and predicaments, Biblical characters and personalities from Abraham, whom God called "His friend" (Isaiah 41:8, James 2:23) and the father of many nations, (Genesis 17:4) to Daniel cast into the den of lions because he refused King Darius' order to stop praying, (Daniel chapter 6) to the three Hebrew boys—Shadrach, Meshach, and Abednego—who were cast into the fiery furnace for refusing to bow down to the golden image of King Nebuchadnezzar, (Daniel chapter 3) to you and me today, roadblocks have always been and always will darken our paths.

We don't have to succumb or ever give in to them because we have the presence of God in our lives through the indwelling Holy Spirit, who is greater than any obstacle we might ever confront or contend with anytime, and anywhere (1st John 4:4).

In conclusion, the invaluable lessons that we learn while struggling, fighting, and contending with our own roadblocks, regardless of whatever they might be, include courage, faith in God's divine direction and plan, a willingness to trust Him completely and unconditionally through devoted tireless acts of perseverance and determination, will ultimately ensure us of one day obtaining and receiving the "prize of the high calling of God through Jesus Christ," which is our "incorruptible crown" of glory, which God Himself will present to me and to you one day for fighting the good fight of faith and overcoming (Philippians 3:12–14, 1st Timothy 6:12)

With God going before me, which He promises that He always will, I have made the conscious decision never to allow roadblocks in life to block or prevent me from receiving the full promise of that which God has for me! (Deuteronomy 31:8).

CHAPTER SIX
"GOD IS ON MY SIDE"

"What, then, shall we say in response to these things? If God is for us, who can be against us?"
(Romans 8:31, NIV)

Perhaps one of the best, or dare I say, the greatest sources of encouragement and inspiration that I have experienced personally throughout this journey of my Christian life, can be found and embodied in the truth of God's Word referenced in the text above: (Romans 8:31) "If God be for us, (me, you) Who can be against us?"

Truthfully, on more occasions than one, God has proven Himself to me more than I can remember throughout my entire lifetime of 72 (seventy-two) years! I have discovered and realized that it was in the times that I suffered my most trying, painful, and personal losses (like the death of my son Michael in the Iraq War in 2007) that I was able to sense and experience the presence of God resonating in my life in ways that mere words could ever express or even begin to convey or explain.

Because of the sovereignty of His love, mercy, and grace, God will never abandon us to the point where we are left alone to fend for ourselves or even attempt to solve life's issues and problems on our own. It doesn't matter how bleak the situation that we are facing might seem to be, nothing is or shall be able to separate us from the power of the love of God (Romans 8:38–39).

Having God always available to be on our side at a moment's notice (as quick as you or I can mutter a prayer) means that without a doubt, the fullness of His power is always going to be there to support us in our most challenging times. When it comes to the subject of Christian Theology, the simple and finer truth of God being on our side as well as being there for us, leads us to four (4) sources of support or evidence found in the book of Romans, Chapter 8, verses 31–39.

Proof number one (1) verse 32 reassures us that God will graciously give us all the things that we might ever need, from the greatest of things to the lesser of things. First and foremost, He (God) did not even spare the sacrifice of His only son (Jesus Christ) to die on the cross of Calvary for our sins that we might have salvation (The greatest gift of all).

Proof number two (2) assures us that there is no charge that can ever be brought against us (by anyone) to point out our fallacies or our weaknesses because it was God himself who declared us righteous in His sight—we are His elect! (Despite our unrighteousness) (v.33)

Proof number three (3) further assures us again that there is no one in heaven or on earth that is capable of ever condemning us (v.34) because Jesus died on the cross, was raised from the dead, and is right now seated at the right hand of God in heaven interceding on our behalf.

Finally, proof number four (4) (v.38–39) boldly makes the declaration that nothing will be able to separate us from the love of God, not even the Devil himself, or all the demons in hell! What more assurance or evidence do we need that "If God is for us and on our side, nothing can be against us?"

The concept of God being on our side is a central theme found in the Word of God, emphasizing that because He (God) is on our side, we have the promise as well as the provision of much-needed assistance, protection, guidance, and direction throughout the course of our lives.

Just because God is on our side, it doesn't mean that in all our present and future endeavors, we are going to have immediate gratification and the answers to all our problems—we won't. There are still going to be mountains and hills to climb, and deep and dark valleys to rise from after experiencing the lowest of times and situations in your life, but when you trust and depend on God, the best is yet to come…I hold fast to and claim this precious promise of God!

Over the past forty years as an educator of literally hundreds of children in elementary, middle school, and high school classes, and having preached hundreds of messages and sermons on Sunday mornings in church worship services, and sadly, officiating funerals, I have often found myself wondering if any of my efforts were helping to change the lives and the situations of anyone.

This year, before classes began at our school (Cleveland Central Catholic High School in Cleveland, Ohio), we hosted a series of pre-enrollment and orientation events where we as educators had the opportunity to meet with parents and prospective students considering enrolling in our school.

A young lady emerged out of the crowd of parents and students, ran up to me, gave me a big hug with a smile on her face, and said: "How are you doing, Mr. Wiggins! You were my seventh-grade teacher in middle school, and I am excited that my fourteen-year-old daughter is going to be one of your new students! I am looking forward to her having the same great experience that I had! You were an awesome teacher as well as a positive role model!"

Two or three more times that evening, this same "impromptu reintroduction" was held with "other former students" who also recognized me as "their teacher" and shared the same sentiments, as they also recognized that their "old teacher" was now also going to be one of their children's teachers!

God again has proven to me that "He is on my side" as He continues to allow me to pour from deep within the reservoir of my soul, those things of intrinsic value that can assist and be of great benefit to the children of this present generation as well as it has been for those who have crossed my path and interacted with me from nearly forty years ago up to today!

I shudder to think about "What if God had not been on or was not on my (or your) side?" In Psalm 124, King David raises this question of contention in the form of a declaration: "If it had not been the Lord who was on our side when men (our enemies) rose up against us," the result for us would have been disastrous!

We would have been "swallowed up" easily by them with the full extent of their wrath and power levied against us, the waters would have overwhelmed us, and we would have drowned!

But we can thank and praise God that because He was and continues to be on our side, we did not become a "prey" to their teeth, and we escaped like a bird from the snare of the prowler whose trap had been broken by the power of God!

Our ultimate source of help and strength remains in the power of the Almighty God our Father, the creator and the sustainer of the heavens and the earth! (my paraphrase!)

The interpretation of Psalm 124 reveals to us that it is an enduring testimony that underscores the extent of God's unfailing love, protection, direction, and deliverance for us, leading us to our destination and disposition that as long as His eternal presence is with us constantly and consistently, there is no way that we cannot make it.

The Bible, in no less than thirty (30) powerful scriptural references that I can both proudly and personally cite, speaks about God's presence in our lives as well as Him being on our side in every good or adverse situation.

This fact alone is a constant reminder that He will provide us with a never-ending source of comfort, strength, guidance, and love that will not end, but bring us peace and the reassurance that we are not alone in this journey of our lives.

In each of these precious passages, the message is soundly and unmistakably clear, regardless of time, place, and situation, from Genesis 28:15 (I am with you and will watch over you wherever you go) to Revelation 21:3 (God's dwelling is among His people).

As believers, you and I can be thankful, rejoice, and be confident that God will always remain faithful to that which He promises us: we will never be left alone, and He is going to be on our side!

It is through and because of such promises that I, as a believer, can continue to hold fast, firm, and true to God's Word because I have that blessed assurance that God will never leave Himself without a witness to testify about just who He is, and what it is that He wants to accomplish in our lives.

A further or deeper exploration of the phrase "God is on my (our) side" for us as Christians, reveals that because we have a closer, more personal and intimate relationship with Him, (God) indicates His very active hand intervening in that which is transpiring and unfolding in our lives daily.

It further suggests to us that we have the assurance that not only is God with us, but that He is working in and through all our circumstances to ultimately please Him as well as give Him all the glory that He alone deserves.

Because "our ways and our thoughts are not the ways and the thoughts of God" (Isaiah 58: 8–9), we don't always know and understand the "whys, the why nots, or the hows or the how comes" of all the specific trials and tribulations that we are experiencing—and have yet to experience in life.

However, knowing that He is true to Himself and the promises of His Word (Romans 8:28), "and we know that all things work together for our good," (those knowing God, and called to His purpose), we can cling tightly and hold firmly to this profound declaration about the goodness of God!

I have witnessed times in my life (I'm sure that most of you have also) when I have found myself asking the question, "Where is the good in this situation?" only to realize that God in His sovereignty has "tailor-made" and orchestrated each step of our lives and simply asks us to trust in Him totally and completely.

In His own time as well as in His own way, God Himself will choose to reveal (or not to reveal) the reasons for what the Apostle Paul refers to as a "light and momentary affliction" that is going to work in and beyond the circumstances that we see, to bring about a far greater good on our behalf! (2nd Corinthians 4:17)

No doubt in my way of thinking (and understanding), it is in this vein that Timothy (the writer of the books of the Bible—1st and 2nd Timothy) offers and gives us the much-needed encouragement and advice that we should persevere and "endure hardness as good soldiers" of Jesus Christ, because it will result in two amazing conclusions: God will be pleased, and it will again work or manifest itself for our good (2nd Timothy 2:3–5).

I find myself (as well as many others do also) wrestling and struggling with the issue of wanting to know all of the reasons that God would allow suffering, hardship, frustration, and pain to come into my life instead of just accepting the fact that He alone knows what's best for me, and all that I have to do is accept (by faith) His predestined, predetermined plan and will for my life.

Our human inquisitive nature to a fault just wants to know why, and even out of our frustration, sometimes we have the audacity to even defiantly demand of God that He tell us, and God simply and lovingly says to us, "Trust me, my child."

Ironically, as I am in the midst of writing this particular portion of this book, it is now nineteen years (January 23, 2007) since two soldiers from the United States Army came to our house, knocked on our front door, and informed us of the sudden and tragic death of our son Michael in Iraq.

People today still approach us (my family) and ask the question: "How do you deal with and prepare for such devastating, life-changing news as the death of your only son?" Our only answer continues to be firmly and resolutely, "You simply trust God."

By and because of the grace of God, my family and I are at peace with Michael's death, but still from the depths of our souls, periodically, there arises the aching, penetrating, painful question: "Why, Lord God, did You allow this to happen to us?"

No sooner than I think this thought, I'm convicted and humbled when I recall the tragic stories from two life-altering events that occurred in the life of Horatio Spafford in 1871 and 1873, respectively. Spafford was a successful Christian businessman and attorney, an avid supporter of D.L. Moody, the renowned founder of the Moody Bible Institute in Chicago, Illinois.

In 1871, the Great Chicago Fire consumed and destroyed a great part of the city of Chicago, including most (if not all) of the property owned by Horatio

Spafford. Two years after settling the business affairs of his great financial loss from this historic fire, Spafford planned a vacation trip to England with his wife and four daughters to join his good friend D.L. Moody, who was scheduled to preach throughout the country.

Spafford arranged for his wife and four daughters to travel by ship a few days ahead of himself, planning to meet them later in England. On that fateful day of November 23, 1873, Spafford's wife Anna and four young daughters (Annie, 12 years old, Maggie, 7 years old, Bessie, four years old, and Tanetta, 18 months old), along with two hundred and twenty-six other passengers on board, drowned when their boat was struck by an iron shipping vessel.

A short time after this tragic event, Horatio received a somber, harrowing telegram from his wife Anna, which simply stated: "I alone survived." A few days after finally reconnecting with his wife in England, Horatio Spafford penned the words to one of the greatest hymns of our Christian Faith—**It Is Well With My Soul.**

I wonder how many of us today, after coming to grips with the reality of what transpired in the life of Horatio Spafford, could give the testimony, "It is well with my soul," after experiencing the worst of times in our own lives?

God blessed Horatio Spafford and his wife Anna with three more children after the death of his four daughters, though seven years after their tragic loss of 1873, four-year-old Horatio Jr. died of Scarlet Fever in November of 1880.

It seems as if tragedy continued to follow the life of Spafford and his wife, Anna (and it does for us in the same way today).

In part, some of the words from this classic hymn convey a deep, abiding, unshakeable faith in God: "When peace like a river, attendeth my way, when sorrows like sea billows roll, whatever my lot thou hast taught me to say, it is well, it is well with my soul!"

It is likely that most of us in our lives will probably never suffer anything that can even begin to compare to the great financial, physical, and emotional losses of Horatio Spafford and his wife, Anna, on those dreadful days years ago.

Years later, before he died in 1888 at the age of fifty-nine, Horatio Spafford and his wife had relocated to Jerusalem, adopted a teenage boy named Jacob, and began a Christian philanthropic group of thirteen adults and three teenagers, ironically nicknamed "The Overcomers."

In the year 2023, the one hundred fiftieth anniversary of the writing of Spafford's beloved hymn (It Is Well With My Soul) was celebrated. Today, churches throughout the United States and around the world still sing this hymn, attesting to the goodness of God that can be birthed out of the most tragic of events that can take place in anyone's life.

What an awesome, amazing story and testimony of faith in God that continues to encourage people like you and me today as we also experience great tragedies and weather the storms of never-ending difficulties in our lives.

Regardless of what we might ever experience or contend with during our lives, we know beyond all shadow of a doubt (at least I do) that God is on our side.

As long as He is on our side, we can remain assured and confident that there is no one or nothing (in heaven above, on earth, or below its surface) that can rise or come against us with the intent or the purpose of trying to overthrow us, to hold us down, or to hold us back.

I rejoice in the fact that God is for me and that He makes the bold proclamation that He is on my side! Why not join me today in realizing the fact that if you have not celebrated His presence in your life, and haven't realized that He also wants to be on your side, you are no doubt missing out on the greatest of blessings that can be extended to us from God Himself. What are you waiting for to accept Him? What do you have to lose?

CHAPTER SEVEN
"NEVER ALONE"

"Be strong and courageous. Do not be afraid or terrified because of them, for the Lord your God goes before you; he will never leave you nor forsake you."
(Deuteronomy 31:6, NIV)

I believe that one of the worst experiences or feelings that anyone can have in their lives is being alone. The state of loneliness brings about a pain that cannot easily be described, explained, or expressed in words.

There have been times in my life that regardless of who might have been around me physically like my wife, (incidentally she is my best and closest of friends) even my mother and my father in the time that they were alive and present in my life, my brothers or my sisters, and any other persons I have viewed or considered as being a part of my "inner circle of friends," feelings of loneliness have still prevailed in my life.

Sometimes, from my perspective, I have viewed the condition or the state of loneliness much in the same manner that David addresses in his most classic writing recorded in the 23rd Psalm, particularly verse 4: "Yea though I walk through the valley of the shadow of death."

Thank God that before David proceeds further into the throes of loneliness, frustration, hopelessness, and despair, he goes on to share that even when he feels this way, there is a bright gleam of help and hope: "I will fear no evil because thou (God, my Lord, my Savior, my Redeemer, my Protector, My Deliverer, My Eternal Friend) art with me." True to His promise, God will never leave us alone!

It is in these times that we find ourselves (often because of our mental, emotional, physical, and even spiritual circumstances or conditions due to our present-day struggles) under the relentless, never-ending attacks of our "Great Adversary" (The Devil, 1st Peter 5:8).

His intent is to deprive us of our joy (John 10:10: "There is one who comes to steal, to kill, and to destroy us by any means necessary"). The method here, which is very effective, is to lead us continuously down and through the path of loneliness.

For us as Christians, God's presence is always guaranteed to be with us because one of His many amazing characteristics and attributes is the promise of Him being the "Omnipresent God" in our lives and all our circumstances. He promises to be forever present with us through the indwelling of His Holy Spirit in our hearts.

In the book of Jeremiah, chapter 23, verses 23 and 24 (GNT), God boldly declares and proclaims Himself as "The God who is everywhere all the time and not limited to being in only one place." His presence with us is a recurring theme throughout the Scriptures that offer us both comfort and peace, which we desperately need in times we are overwhelmed, isolated, and alone.

Personally, I have always been a lover of many original hymns of our Christian faith that consistently and effectively convey the power of God through His presence in our lives, offering us a sense of great solace, comfort, and much-needed peace in times of "storms."

One such hymn (Never Alone), attributed to writer Ludie B. Pickett in 1897, offers God's promise of His never-ending presence in our lives—especially in our most challenging times. The words from the iconic first verse of this hymn resonate within my soul whenever I hear or sing this song: "I've seen the lightning flashing, and heard the thunder roll, I've felt sin's breakers dashing, which tried to conquer my soul. I heard the voice of my Savior bidding me still to fight on, He promised never to leave me, never to leave me alone!"

Finally, the words from the refrain give us a sense of everlasting comfort and the reassurance of peace to our souls: "No never alone, no never alone, He promised never to leave me, never to leave me alone. No, never alone, no never alone, He promised never to leave me, never to leave me alone!"

Even when God is present in our lives (and He always is), it is still possible for us to feel as if we are alone. However, when we as believers experience being alone, there are at least five things that we should consider as our course of action:

Number 1. It is most important that we spend some time meditating on the presence of God in our lives. The 134th Psalm, in addition to the book of Hebrews chapter 13 and verse 5, consistently reminds and encourages us that wherever we are, and whatever we are experiencing, God promises us that He will always be on our side.

2. In times that we find ourselves alone, it is important that we spend time in prayer because prayer connects us to and with God. (Isaiah 41:10, 1st Peter 5:7). In doing this, we will find and experience comfort and peace of mind in talking to and with Him.

3. Strength can be found (despite our circumstances) by sharing our faith in God with our fellow brothers and sisters in Christ (Hebrews 10:24–25, Psalm 133:1).

4. As we continue to face times of being alone, we need to trust completely in God's plan for our lives and rely upon the strength that He promises us (Jeremiah 29:11, Proverbs 3:5–6).

5. Finally, if we commit ourselves to resting in the Holy Spirit, He will continue to sustain us with His peace and comfort (Isaiah 26:3)

Many times in my life, I have had to face the heavy burden of believing that I was all alone. I can vividly recall my first encounter with loneliness or being alone. My parents divorced when I was just about seven or eight years old. When I look back at this time in my life, it was a very difficult time. Even now (today), I get a bit teary-eyed when I recall this time in my life.

Mentally, physically, and emotionally, I was a wreck! It was not until I was nearly thirty years old that a good friend and neighbor (the late Mrs. Bernice Lavender) shared with me her perspective on my decorum as she noticed me sitting on the front steps of my house from the front porch of her home across the street.

Over forty years ago, I painstakingly recall her account of what she observed as she witnessed me as a lonely, scared young child wrestling with the harsh reality of my parents' divorce. In her own words, Mrs. Lavender shared this poignant analysis of her thoughts and impressions of my state of mind and being:

"My prayers went out for you much more than you could ever think or imagine. Your world was torn apart because I know that as a young boy, you deeply loved your mother (little boys do), and your parents' divorce literally "ripped" her out of your life, and there was nothing that you could do about it.

"Many times, I thought that you wanted to run away—and was surprised and relieved that you never did. You simply had no idea where to run, who to turn to, or what to do. You were very vulnerable, hurt, helpless, lonely, and alone. My prayer was that somehow and some way, God Himself would pick up the broken and shattered pieces of your life, put them back together again, and make you a whole and productive person.

"Today," she concluded, "I see the man that God has allowed you to become. You have, by His grace, weathered the 'storm' of your parents' divorce, and are on your way to becoming the man that God wants you to become. I wish you well as you begin your journey into marriage…"

What powerful words of encouragement, support, and love these were from a beautiful, precious Christian woman who has known me most of my life. Just about two years ago, Mrs. Lavender died at the age of ninety years old and went home to be with the Lord! What an impact her presence in my life has made, confirming the reality that God will never and does never leave us alone to bear the burdens of life by ourselves. He is always going to place someone in our lives to affirm His support, and His presence will always be there for us.

When I fast forward my heart, my mind, and my thoughts from this first episode of being lonely, hurt, confused, and alone in my life, I can't help but focus on and relive another very painful episode from my life.

On January 23, 2007, my wife and I suddenly and tragically lost our only son, Staff Sergeant Michael J. Wiggins, in the Iraq War. What I can share with anyone now is the fact that there could possibly be no pain, no amount of emotional suffering, or the heart-wrenching reality anywhere that can be compared to that of losing a child.

Yes, it is true that the emotional distress and the grief associated with the loss of a child surpass any other fear or pain of suffering that one might ever experience in their lifetime. For us, our son was a bright and rising star—on the cusp of just beginning to realize his full God-given potential as a young man. What a promising future he had. Of course, the news of Mike's death completely and utterly devastated us! It took us to the lowest depths of anger, despair, frustration, and pain imaginable, one associated with sleepless nights and streams of never-ending tears.

Even though we were surrounded by an endless flow of "well-wishers," including throngs of visits from neighbors, family members, friends, pastors, and even complete strangers—from the mayor of several neighboring cities, to the Governor of the State of Ohio (Ted Strickland at this time in 2007) to Congresswoman the late Stephanie Tubbs Jones—we still felt hopeless, lonely, and alone, especially when Michael's death was no longer the "hot news" of the day. Every day, cards filled up my mailbox from all around the country, but I still felt as if no one cared—I was all alone.

Thank God for the presence and the support of a small, loud, dynamo of a preacher (the late pastor Robert L. Ferguson) who came to my house, sat in my basement, held my hand, and cried an endless flow of tears with me without ever saying one word. This vigil lasted literally for several hours, and now, even some nineteen years later, people still ask me, "What was it that you and Pastor Ferguson talked about?"

I smile and respond, "Nothing," as I realized that at that moment, following the passing of my son, I would not have to endure the pain alone. Thank God for being faithful and true to His promise from His Word that He would never leave us to be forsaken, especially at one of the lowest points in our lives.

God knew that all I needed was for someone (Pastor Ferguson) to show up and let me know that He (God) was still the ever-present help and support that I needed, and He did that and more through the presence and the support of this man (Psalm 46:1).

Although it has taken a great deal of time (time indeed spent in God's presence will put an end to pain and heal it), I continue to find great solace and relief in God's Word.

The comforting, soothing, reassuring words from Isaiah 41:10 remain a beacon of sustaining hope and support for me: "Fear not, for I am with you, be not dismayed, for I am your God, I will strengthen you, I will help you, I will uphold you with my right hand of righteousness."

For me and my family, it has been in and through our times of experiencing loneliness and the thought of being alone that we have realized that it has been through God's Word that we have come to understand that His presence in our lives allows us to not only understand loneliness, but to appreciate the fact that we can rejoice in the assurance of His never-ending presence, love, and support that ultimately we will continue to have His comforting guidance in our lonely times to "whisper" words of comfort and peace.

Because of God's commitment and His promise to "never leave me alone," one thing remains true in my life, and it is crystal clear that even during great adversity, hurt, conflict, and pain, "the best is yet to come," and I am claiming this awesome promise of God in my life!

Chapter Eight
"I Will Still Rise"

"Now will I arise," says the Lord.
"Now I will be exalted, now will I be lifted up."
(Isaiah 33:10, NIV)

I have come to the realization, as well as the understanding, that God, in His own time and in His own way, born out of my need for necessity, will decisively come into my situation to intervene on my behalf. Why? Because He has a plan for my life (and yours as well) (Jeremiah 29:11) that He alone knows. This plan, though it is sometimes difficult to understand, is to help me, not to hurt me, to give me directions, and a promise that will be full of hope and success for my future!

"That expected end," as some believe in Jeremiah 29:11, doesn't necessarily center upon or focus its attention solely or primarily upon material and financial prosperity, because God is not limited, confined to, or obligated to bless me in this manner. There is much more to God "rising up" on my behalf. I am glad that there is!

Personally, I have claimed the promise of Isaiah 33:10 that He (God himself) will indeed arise to execute His divine judgment against all who oppose me and the plan that He has for my life. They (those opposing me and His plan for my life) have no authority, no power, or no control over whatever it is that God has in plan and in store for me.

Sometimes I have found that in life (many of you will agree) that the pressure, as well as the unrelenting issues, trials, uncertainties, and the challenges of life, whatever they might be, often leave us crushed, broken, and beaten down to the point that we feel as if we will never rise again.

However, it is in these times that God always positions Himself to show up in my life—and things change! It is important for us to understand that there are many benefits available to us because we are the children of God. One significant benefit is God's promise to provide care for us from the attacks of our enemies.

It is certainly advantageous to us (believers) to strive to live a righteous life as opposed to living one that has an evil or "wicked" consequence. Make no mistake about it or fail to realize one simple fact: "We are all going to fall at some point in our lives."

After we fall, however, the question is, "What do we do?" Do we wallow around in self-pity and make weak excuses for why we fell, or do we put forth every effort to rise again?

According to Proverbs 24:16, a righteous person will fall seven times (and get up), meaning that he (she) may continue in their lives to fall repeatedly but won't stay down. Learning to lean, to trust, and to depend on God throughout our lives when we fall puts us in the position to call upon His grace as well as His strength.

If we are to continue to fight the good fight of faith as soldiers (1st Timothy 6:12), even when we fall, we have been afforded the opportunity of being able to rise again because the power of God is present in our lives. His presence is a constant, consistent reminder that His strength and undying support are always available to us.

One of the greatest accomplishments that we can ever make in our lives lies not in the fact that we all fall, but rather that we rise every time that we fall. A person who never tries to stand up, especially for what is right, is always going to fall.

As I am writing this particular chapter of this book (The Best is Yet To Come), we are currently celebrating Black History Month in the United States (February, 2025). My attention, ironically, was drawn to a classic poem published by the late great African American author and civil rights activist Maya Angelou in 1978: **And Still I Rise.**

This poem stands as a beacon of hope, help, and light to generations of African Americans who, for many centuries, have literally had their hopes, dreams, and aspirations "pressed down" and crushed to the ground by systematic racism, blatant discrimination, and a society that wouldn't allow us to thrive even though we have distinguished ourselves and accomplished great things.

Yet today, I can attest personally that by faith in God, we have risen to the greatest of heights and accomplished amazing things as a race of people! We as Christians, believers, and followers of God through and because of Jesus Christ, regardless of our race, creed, or gender, are going to constantly be challenged with and by situations in our lives where our Great Adversary (The Devil Himself) will continue to place us in precarious situations that will work against us to crush our faith and trust in God.

However, because of the promises of God and the encouragement that we have from His Word, we find the resiliency, the redemption, and the hope of His never-ending love and support for us, which gives us the ability to still rise.

The challenges of adversity for most of us (both Christians and non-Christians alike) can often be overwhelming. It is encouraging for us to realize that we need to lean upon our faith in God during these tough and difficult times.

In the word of God (Psalm 55:22), we are challenged and called to "cast all of our burdens on the Lord" because He has promised us that He will sustain us and never allow us to succumb to those things that cause us to fall (and we will). However, when we do fall, we have the assurance (Psalm 46:1) that God is not only our refuge, but He is also the source of strength that will serve as a "very present hope" in our troubled times.

Just knowing this brings us much-needed comfort, peace, and joy when we find ourselves pressed down under the weight of our burdens, knowing that because of Him, we will rise again and again triumphantly over all types of adversity.

Though college for me represented a formidable challenge, I am very proud of the fact that by the grace of God, I was one of (if not) the first of the Wiggins' family to obtain a Bachelor's, a Master's, and a Doctorate degree!

One of the proudest moments of my life was receiving my bachelor's degree in education from Ashland University in 1974, with my grandfather, the late James Wiggins, the patriarch of my family, in attendance.

This accomplishment continues to both inspire and motivate me today because my grandfather could neither read nor write! As a family, we have truly "come this far by faith," leaning, trusting, and depending on the Lord, who has, as the song continues to say, never failed us yet!

As I proudly look at my family today, we are still rising and being "lifted up" by the power of God! Now I have a deeper, more abiding respect, appreciation, and understanding for the "Black National Anthem" **(Lift Every Voice and Sing)** written by James Weldon Johnson in 1900.

The words in part are: "Lift every voice and sing, 'til earth and heaven ring, ring with the harmonies of liberty, let our rejoicing rise, high as the listening skies, let it resound loud as the rolling sea. Sing a song full of the faith that the dark past has taught us, sing a song full of the hope that the present has brought us, facing the rising sun, of our new day begun, let us march on 'til victory is won."

Symbolically contained within this "poem" (song) written by this amazing black man one hundred and twenty-five years ago, is a message of faith, hope, and a belief in God that anyone (not just a black race of people) who has been oppressed or treated unjustly by that which has transpired in their lives which inevitably was not in their hands, can and will rise from the depths of doubt and despair to ascend to heights that only God himself can allow them to envision!

To 'rise again" in the eyes of God is a constant, consistent reality as well as a reminder to us as believers that we are promised the opportunity of being renewed by God Himself to the point that with His help and presence in our lives, we can and will overcome all of the challenges of life and make positive, meaningful strides forward to becoming all that God has promised and intended for us to become and to accomplish. Never give up hope!

The Apostle Paul expresses this dilemma (2nd Corinthians 4:8–10) that we as Christians wrestle and struggle with every day of our lives: "We are hard pressed on every side, but not crushed, perplexed, but not in despair, persecuted, but not abandoned, struck down, but not destroyed because we always carry around in our body the death of Jesus, so that the life of Jesus may also be revealed in our body."

Even in our most fearful and weakest of moments, we are going to experience times of suffering just as Jesus Himself suffered. We are encouraged to never give up hope (lose heart) even in the face of defeat because by the power of God revealed to us in the resurrection of Jesus Christ from the grave, victory can and will become ours—we have the blessed assurance that we will rise figuratively and literally from the adversity that has us bound!

Life has and will continue to present us with an array of challenges that we must face, but we still must know and understand that God, in and through the promises of His Word, offers us that which is a solid foundation upon which we can stand, even amid uncertainties and an ever-changing world of doubt and fear.

Our reading, understanding, and the application of biblical truths to our lives, goes a long way in helping us to create a spirit of empowerment from God, who alone gives us the determination to remain committed to His Word as the only real source of strength as we continue to press toward the mark for the prize of the high calling of God in Jesus Christ (Philippians 3:14).

Ultimately, for us as Christians, "the prize" is the incorruptible crown of life, righteousness, and the eternal glory of God that will not fade away under any circumstances. It is what God has called us to and for, and the reason that we rise after falling is that it is the reward we stand to receive at the culmination of this journey of our lives.

God knew in His predestined plan and will for our lives that we were going to face great difficulty as we pressed for and pursued this prize, but through His mercy and grace, He prepared us by implanting within us all of the spiritual blessings and the gifts that we would ever need in order to accomplish his purpose.

I love to draw a renewed sense of support and strength from one of Paul's many words of encouragement again to all believers found in Hebrews 12:1–2 NIV: "Therefore, since we are surrounded by such a great cloud of witnesses, let us throw off everything that hinders and the sin that so easily entangles. And let us run with perseverance, the race marked out for us. Let us fix our eyes on Jesus, the pioneer and perfecter of faith."

In other words, we are called to put forth every effort to live a life of faith that God Himself has called us to live with joy, though we know that this life itself was never promised to us as being easy. However, we can rejoice in knowing that Jesus himself, our Lord and Savior, is seated at the right hand of God, praying and interceding on our behalf that we might indeed make it. Because he has overcome, we also can rejoice in knowing that we, too, shall overcome.

In addition, a "great cloud of witnesses" (those who have already completed their race) is standing and cheering for us, proclaiming that we can also make it because they already have made it, by the grace and the power of God!

As a final word of encouragement to all of us (you and me), true believers and followers of Jesus Christ know that when we fall and sit in darkness, the God of our Salvation will not allow our enemies to rejoice over us. He will help us to arise and will provide Himself as a light for us to brighten our path! (Micah 7:8)

CHAPTER NINE
"HEARING THE VOICE OF GOD"

"Call to me and I will answer you. I'll tell you marvelous and wondrous things that you could never figure out on your own."
(Jeremiah 33:3, MSG)

Have you ever heard the voice of God? How do you know it was Him? How did He sound? What did He say? Hearing the voice of God for a Christian implies that for us to hear Him (God), a person must be attuned to listening and to obeying that which God has to say.

The primary method for us to "hear" God's voice is through the committed process of both reading and studying His Word on a regular basis, and then not only obeying it, but also beginning to make a practical application of scriptural truths to our lives.

I believe that God has always regularly and consistently talked to His people throughout time, but far too often, we miss the opportunity of hearing His message because we do not regularly seek out His guidance and direction for our lives. Usually, it is at a time of us being in a crisis or experiencing some difficulty or the need to make a major decision in our lives before we seek Him out.

Hearing God's voice must begin with us having an internal experience on our part that is composed of our feelings, our beliefs, our convictions, and any impressions that we have that closely align themselves with how well we understand not only God's teachings, but also His character as well.

Developing a mindset and a "heart" for hearing God's voice comes about as we commit ourselves to a close relationship with Him by focusing on how to position ourselves to listen to His voice for guidance as well as for direction. It is imperative that we learn to distinguish God's voice for ourselves apart from the many voices calling out to us from the chaos and the lies of a confused world of deceptive voices, namely that of the Devil himself.

John 10:27 proclaims a profound biblical truth that reflects one of the basic teachings of Jesus Christ: "My sheep hear my voice. They know me and follow me." This passage of scripture underscores and speaks to a deep connection that exists between him (our Savior) and his followers (disciples).

This spiritual discernment is born out of an intimate relationship that must be forged between the believers and their leader (Jesus Christ). Without this relationship, we cannot possibly hear the voice of God speaking to us today. It is because of this relationship that we are empowered to hear the voice of God.

There are essentially many ways that God speaks to us, but I am only going to highlight five (5) ways that He speaks to us, His children, today: First and foremost, God speaks to us through His Word. It is through His Word that scripture comes alive in our eyes with the ability to address our specific needs and situations.

In 2nd Timothy 3:16, we read that "all scripture is given by the inspiration of God and is profitable to us for teaching, for reproof, for correction, and for instruction in righteousness, with the intent of equipping us as men and women of God with all that we need to accomplish good works.

In God's Word, we find all that we need to impact our lives and make a difference. The second way that God speaks to us is through His witnesses from one believer to another. It is through the indwelling of the Holy Spirit that God speaks to all who have a relationship with Him.

Because of this, God can and does speak through a sense of wise counsel from one believer to another. As He speaks to us through these witnesses, we can effectively spread His love and our faith in Him with others around us. Luke

12:12 says that the Holy Spirit Himself will teach us those things that we ought to say to one another.

The third way that God chooses to speak to us is through the "world" of our life's circumstances. Remember that God is present in all of our situations and circumstances, whether we view them as good or bad.

Ultimately, in each situation we find ourselves in, God always sees us, cares for us, and is always going to speak to us. He uses various circumstances and situations in our everyday experiences that will lead us to a place to hear His voice.

It could be the experience of a personal loss, 2nd Samuel 12:16–23 (David's loss of a young son), it could be through a situation that He chooses to deliver us from, Daniel chapter 6 (Daniel delivered from the lion's den), or it could be the special favor that He extends to us, His children, Psalm 5.

The fourth way that I want us to consider how God speaks to us is through the witness of His creation. Certainly, God has created a masterpiece of beauty in all of creation.

One simply views the majestic mountains, hearing the roaring voice of a mighty lion, smelling the sweet fragrance of a red rose, and the powerful, destructive force of a hurricane or a tornado (Psalm 19:1–2).

Finally, (the fifth way that we are considering that God speaks to us), it is through the realm of prayer that God speaks to us. Therein lies one of many reasons that He (God) constantly calls and encourages us to pray without ceasing (1st Thessalonians 5:16–17).

Prayer is the avenue through which we convey to God our heartfelt thoughts, feelings, fears, dreams, frustrations, and aspirations. In return, He promises to not only hear that which is weighing upon our hearts and minds, but to also respond according to His own will.

Prayer should not be misconstrued as a one-sided monologue of us as believers communicating to God, but rather a dialogue in which we can connect to God in an open and sharing manner, in which He, in turn, speaks back to us with much-needed instruction and direction for our lives.

Regardless of how God speaks to us, we should hear His voice loud and clear—as long as we are in fellowship with Him, and we respond (hopefully) by doing that which He has called us to do. We know that He alone has the key to the plan for each of our lives (Jeremiah 29:11).

In a world that is so full of "noise" and many voices competing for our attention, it is hard for us to hear God's voice speaking to us. In our lives, we become very busy even when we are "working for God" by serving Him through the service that we provide to so many other people.

It becomes very crucial and critical for us as Christians during our "daily walk" that we learn how to hear the voice of God. We are lost without hearing Him speak to us for guidance and direction. For us, hearing God's voice means that we must be able to listen carefully for His directions, instructions, and guidance.

We cannot hear God speak if we don't first believe that He speaks to us today. (Many people don't believe that He does) Jeremiah 33:3 encourages us to "call out to God", and He promises to not only answer us, but to show us things that we have no idea about.

We can't hear God's voice speaking to us if we don't "belong to Him." Belonging to Him means that we have been saved by His grace through our faith alone in Jesus Christ (Ephesians 2:8–9).

More importantly, we hear His voice when we spend time studying and reading His Word (The Bible) and by both contemplating and meditating our thoughts upon it. The more time that we spend engaging in this process, the easier it becomes for us to recognize His voice.

If our actions go contrary to what we have read and studied from His Word, we can rest assured that we have not heard His voice. The voice of God speaking to us is never going to contradict that which is contained in His Word. The very Word of God itself is truth (John 17:17).

For me personally, my life of forty (40) plus years in ministry places me in a position that allows me to be a direct witness of hearing God's voice speak to me.

In 1982, I "answered" the formal call of God into a life of ministry (spreading the Gospel of Jesus Christ). God "spoke to me" specifically and directly through His Word, through the witness of other people playing a crucial role in my life, and through the world of circumstances that I encountered before I finally acknowledged my calling and submitted myself humbly and faithfully to ministry, and have not turned back!

There have been at least two other times in my life that God spoke to me and called me into areas of ministry that have totally impacted and changed my life.

First, in 1988, after spending some twenty-five years serving in various positions (from Sunday School teacher, Sunday School Superintendent, to time as a deacon, and as a minister) at the Good Shepherd Baptist Church in Cleveland, Ohio, under the leadership of the late Rev. Dr. Eddie L. Hawkins, I sensed God calling me to the position of Assistant Pastor at the Bright Star Missionary Baptist Church, also in Cleveland, Ohio, under the leadership of Rev. Dr. David Hunter.

I served faithfully in this position at Bright Star for eighteen years until 2006, when God called me to begin a new church ministry (Friends Fellowship Bible Church, in Cleveland, Ohio, where I have served as the founding Senior Pastor for the past nineteen years! (still serving presently in 2025)

Recently, I came across an article written by Ben Mandrell in **Lifeway Voices (Church Ministry and Leadership**) published on February 17, 2020. In this article, Mandrell recounts that **there are three things guaranteed to happen when the voice of God calls you.** After reading this article, I must say that I wholeheartedly agree with his findings.

Guarantee number one says: When the voice of God calls you, you simply won't have any idea of where it is that He is going to take you. Certainly, for me, this was the case. All I could do (and have done) was to prepare myself, and when God called, I had no idea or even the slightest clue of where I was going over the course of my now forty years in ministry.

Guarantee number two says: When the voice of God calls you, you will feel ill-equipped or unprepared for that which He has called you to. Sure, I had some formal education and skills, but there was a tremendous gap between my skills and my education. Mandrell says that this gap represents the space that allows your faith to grow. He was right, and my faith in God did grow into this gap.

Guarantee number three advises or informs us that you will (and I did) experience a unique filling of the Holy Spirit in your assignment that will fulfill your calling in and with the strength of the Lord.

Throughout the times that we (you and I) have heard the voice of God speaking to us and calling out to us to commit ourselves to some type of service for Him, we must continue to prepare ourselves for that which is often unexpected and embrace the faith that we have in God in order to complete that which He has called us to do.

From the "beginning" (In The book of Genesis), the voice of God was present in creation. All of heaven and earth responded to His voice when He simply spoke everything into existence through His voice. In the first chapter of Genesis, God simply spoke the words through His voice, "Let there be light, (Genesis 1:3), and light as we know it came into existence in the form of night and day.

In Genesis 1:6–26, God said, "Let there be a firmament (heaven) and earth (land)." And both came into existence. From there, God called great bodies of water (oceans, lakes, rivers, seas), as well as every form of tree and plant, and all living things on earth (from animals to insects) into being—all of heaven and earth as we now know came forth into existence and being in response to hearing the voice of God!

It is no wonder that in the process of "making and shaping" man in His own (God's) image and likeness, which was His crowning glory of creation, God chose to "talk" to man in a personal, intimate way, and He still does so today!

Man has always communed, talked to, and fellowshipped with God, and this relationship continues as God talks to us through His Word.

Hearing the voice of God is very important to us as Christians because as we hear His voice, it guides and directs us through our daily lives, giving us strength for each day, enhances our faith in Him, and most importantly, it reassures us of His continued presence with us always.

I personally rejoice in knowing that I can hear the voice of God speaking to me through my time spent with Him in prayer, through the reading and the studying of His Word, and through the practical application of its truths to my life, and through the presence of the indwelling Holy Spirit in my life.

When God speaks and we respond to His voice, things begin to happen in our lives because His words carry divine authority as well as dictate the very purpose for our being, which is to honor and to glorify Him in all that we do.

As Jeremiah 33:3 states, "I have called out to God, and not only has he answered me as he promised that he would do from his word, but he has begun to show me great and wonderful things that I simply had no idea would ever be possible."

My prayer is that He will allow me (and you) to remain open to hearing His voice and responding in a manner that would honor and glorify Him above all else that we do in our lives.

CHAPTER TEN
"I'VE COME TOO FAR"

"Commit your way to the Lord, trust also in Him, and He shall bring it to pass."
(Psalm 37:5, NKJV)

On April 25, 2000, the classic gospel singing group (duo) (Mary, Mary), composed of sisters Erica and Tina Campbell, wrote and released one of their first of many significant songs, at least in my opinion, entitled **I Just Can't Give Up Now.** The lyrics of this song have encouraged, inspired, and motivated countless number of people (including me) to continue their road of fighting "the good fight of faith" along the journey of their lives.

In part, the lyrics of this song say: "I just can't give up now, I've come too far from where I started from. Nobody told me the road would be easy, and I don't believe He's brought me this far to leave me."

Verse 1 goes on to share a message about the struggles of life that we all face. "There will be mountains that I will have to climb, there will be battles that I will have to fight, but victory or defeat, it's up to me to decide. How can I expect to win if I never try?"

"I just can't give up now"!

For me personally, this song that I have listened to for the past twenty-five (25) years has put my life in a much better perspective and context than I could have ever imagined. I have come away believing as well as expecting that God, certainly over the past seventy-plus years of my life, didn't bring me this far to leave me! By and because of my faith in Him, I have come a long way!

I'm convinced now more than ever **that the best is yet to come!** I'm looking for and expecting God to do even more!

Usually, whenever someone proclaims that "they have come too far," it shares some insight about a struggle that has occurred in their lives that they have overcome and progressed to a place and a point in time where they have no intention of quitting or turning back!

Looking back over my life, I can literally be a witness and testify about how good God has been in His promise to not only sustain me, but to keep me moving forward in my life's journey in pursuit of what He has providentially planned for me to accomplish.

No, it hasn't been easy, and no one has "given me" anything that I have not worked hard to earn—it was and has been the grace of God that has guided, protected, and directed me up to and through this present time. Without His (God's) ever-abiding presence in my life, there is no way that I would have ever made it.

No, I just can't give up now because I've come too far from where I started. I've been told, and I know that it takes both sunshine and rain to make flowers grow. God, in His all-wise, all-knowing omniscience, allows "storms" to come into our lives for many reasons. These struggles cause our faith to mature and to grow.

These storms in nature can be physical, emotional, or spiritual challenges, serving to bring us to a time of repentance, to temper our faith and trust in God, to refine our character, or just to teach us how to trust in God more deeply.

I've come to realize that it is the challenges and the trials that we experience in our lives that God uses as a vehicle to draw us closer to Him and the principles or the standards that He has for our lives. Sometimes in life, we allow ourselves to get "caught up" in situations that have led us to make sinful choices.

Yet, even in our willful choices (disobedience) to do the wrong thing, we discover that God is always present with us and will draw us back to Him in repentance. Through the trials and the challenges that we experience, we are sometimes forced to rely upon God's strength rather than to trust in the limitations of our own.

Ultimately, this results in us growing spiritually as we learn to endure, persevere, and in time, submit to the will and the way of God as we grow to become more like our Savior, Jesus Christ.

As we weather the storms in our lives, it gives us a more accurate perspective of just who God is and how He wants to work in our lives. As we conquer storms with the help of God, we come away with a better understanding of how and what He has brought us through.

It is during this time that we realize and appreciate His strength in our lives, and the sufficiency of the impact that His saving grace has made upon each of us.

At various times in our lives, I think that each of us should take a deep, serious look at where we started from, how we started, and see just how far we have progressed.

The only life that I have ever known is and has always been closely aligned with growing up in a Christian home and environment. I can't ever remember a time in my life when I didn't attend church services and Sunday School on a regular basis.

Thankfully, I was raised in a Christian home where the principles, as well as all the fundamental doctrines of the Bible and the Christian faith, were not only taught to me but were modeled and lived in front of me as the conduit of how to live a god-fearing, spirit-filled life.

This alone has made all the difference in my life, and the result is that I would not be "the man of God" that I am today if not for this "spiritual intervention" in my formative years.

To say that life has been a real challenge as well as a struggle is not an attempt to minimize the scope of the road that I have traveled down. I've learned that anything worth having is worth fighting for.

When I pause and think about the phrase "I've come too far from where I started," my mind invariably turns to the gospel of Luke chapter 9, and verse 62:

"No man who puts his hand to the plow and turns back is fit for the kingdom of God."

Meaning, that when one decides to put his (or her) "hand to the plow" to involve themselves in a life-long process of advancing the Kingdom of God, it underscores the fact that they have made a long-term commitment to Jesus Christ.

There is no such thing as turning back or giving up because the work of kingdom building by spreading and sharing the Word of God so that others might be saved is not one that should be taken lightly. As our Savior and perfect example, Jesus Himself literally put His "hand to the plow," refused to turn back, and decided to go all the way to Calvary's cross to die for our sins and our redemption.

Have you ever stopped to consider what would have happened if Jesus had "turned back" from His calling of crucifixion on the cross for our sins? Where would you and I be today?

Thank God for the magnitude of the depth of His love for us (Romans 5:8) that even while we yet remain in our sins, Christ died for us! Because of this amazing, unconditional love for us, Jesus honored and kept His "hand to the plow" and suffered, hung, bled, and died on Calvary's cross.

As a result of this unselfish sacrifice of love for me, hopefully and prayerfully for you as well, we have come too far to turn back now and willingly have decided to "present ourselves as living sacrifices" for the work that God has called us to do.

The tremendous cost of our salvation was too great a price and would bring shame and dishonor to Jesus Christ if we were to ever quit, give up, or turn back. The words of a simple but poignant song that I learned many years ago as a young teenager continue to both convict and encourage me even today:

"I have decided to follow Jesus, I have decided to follow Jesus, I have decided to follow Jesus, no turning back, no turning back! Though no one joins me, still I will follow, though no one joins me, still I will follow, though no one joins me, still I will follow, no turning back, no turning back!"

The significance of the phrase "I've come too far" for me as a Christian, in all actuality, seriously expresses a profound sense of two important characteristics or traits we need in order to be successful and productive in our walk of faith in Jesus Christ.

Those two characteristics are determination and perseverance. Both attributes are needed when we experience moments of crisis in our lives as Christians that challenge our faith as well as our commitment to serving the Lord.

With the help of the ever-present Holy Spirit in our lives, despite all of the difficulties that we face, we are ably equipped to navigate our way through whatever snares and traps the enemy (the Devil himself) sets up for us as stumbling blocks or pitfalls.

Perseverance is a committed, continual effort to achieve something despite the challenges and difficulties that have been placed in front of us. There are only two courses of action available. We can either trust God, maintain our faith in Him, or we can quit and abandon hope.

Trusting God fully and completely entails us as believers seeking out the truth that He has laid out in front of us in His Word, spending time with Him in concerted prayer, walking in the light of the Holy Spirit, and waiting in faith for Him to direct our path.

Going further, we must develop and maintain a sense of spiritual determination, which is the ability to make difficult decisions in our lives based on the truths revealed to us in God's Word. This determination must be carried out regardless of whatever resistance we face from our adversary (Satan).

It is in the light of this determination that we must continue to trust in the leading and the direction of God's presence indwelling us through the Holy Spirit to the point that we maintain the course He has set before us until we accomplish His goal and plan for our lives.

I thank and praise God that He alone "knows the plan that He has for me" (and each of you) in our lives. According to Jeremiah 29:11, this plan is to ensure that each of us, as children of God, might have the good, expected plan ending in success sprinkled with thoughts of His peace sustaining us throughout our lives.

As my life continues to unfold before my eyes, I continue to embrace the promise that **the best is yet to come,** and I wholeheartedly accept this promise as the underlying reason that I've come too far from where I started to give up now!

There have been many times during my life, as it relates to my calling into ministry, that I have entertained the thought or the idea of "giving up" because things haven't gone the way that I hoped and planned that they would go. I'm tired! Nothing seems to be working! Nothing seems to be happening! I'm not having (by my own critical assessment) much success! What's the use?

In times like these in the midst of my own personal "pity party" that the Holy Spirit leads me to read again and claim for the "umpteenth time" the promise recorded in Philippians chapter 1, verse 6: "Being confident of this very thing, that he which hath begun a good work in you will perform it until the day of Jesus Christ."

Enough said! Even though I don't always see it, the work that God has called me to is "a good work," and He will continue to give me all that I have and will need in order that this work might be performed until the day of Jesus Christ!

Neither you nor I know when "that day" is going to come, but I do know that all God wants and expects of me (and you) is that we continue to allow ourselves, along with all the talents and the abilities that He has given to us, to "perform it" until the day of Jesus Christ! (Not by might nor by power, but by My Spirit says the Lord—Zechariah 4:6).

When we decide to commit ourselves to the Lord, it ultimately means that everything that is within us, all of our plans, our fears, our hopes, our aspirations, our decisions that we make, and even every burden that we attempt to bear, must be willingly and consciously given to Him as an act of our faith.

Because He cares for us, God will take whatever it is that we have committed to Him and allow it to work together for our good in order that His will is going to be accomplished in our lives.

Regardless of how far we have come, there remain more steps on the path that we have decided to take before we arrive at where God wants us to be.

By and with the help of God, I plan to continue to move forward in my walk of faith, trusting, depending, and believing that I indeed have come too far to quit, to stop, or to turn around.

I intend one day (I hope and I pray by the grace of God) to celebrate and rejoice in the fulfillment of the promise of God that, in spite of all of the difficulties, the disappointments, the adversity, and the pain, the **best is yet to come!**

CHAPTER ELEVEN
"I EXPECT TO WIN"

"But thanks be to God! He gives us the victory through our Lord Jesus Christ."
(1st Corinthians 15:57, NKJV)

There is an "old" classic gospel song written and released by the late Gospel iconic singer, Walter Hawkins, in 1984, entitled **When the Battle is Over.** I love the lyrics in verse one, which in part say: "Don't wait 'til the battle is over, shout now, you know in the end you're gonna win!"

More recently, in this year (2025), great Gospel singer Tamela Mann's recent hit song, which is destined to become a classic one, entitled **I Expect To Win,** puts into perspective my expectation about the journey of my Christian life! After enduring all the struggles, the trials, the pain, and the never-ending adversities of life, with more still to come my way (and your way too), victory is and shall ultimately be mine! (ours).

Oswald Chambers, a great Christian minister, teacher, and author of the early twentieth century, made what I believe is a profound quote about us as Christians receiving and accomplishing victory in our Christian lives. "God can do nothing for me until I recognize the limits of what is humanly possible, allowing Him to do the impossible."

Before it (this Christian life) is all over, **I expect to win** if for no other reason than the declaration made by the Apostle Paul in his epistle (Colossians) chapter 1, verse 27. "Christ in me is the hope of glory."

This "hope of glory" alluded to in this passage of scripture by the Apostle Paul is a forward-looking guarantee or promise that we can be confident with an expectant hope and the knowledge that God is going to reward us with, above all else, a life that will exceed all our imagination, far above the limitations of our earthly existence.

Not only do I expect to win, but I am also going to win! As I look back over the past seventy years of my life, like most people, I have been impacted by seasons and periods of time that have been highlighted by almost an equal number of smatterings of what can be classified as good times and bad times.

Quite naturally, it was in times of experiencing my deepest, darkest, most difficult days that I felt like I would never again see the light of day or even smile again.

Some eighteen years ago (January 23, 2007), my wife and I "lost" our only son (Staff Sergeant Michael J. Wiggins) as he was serving our country faithfully fighting on the battlefields of Bilad, Iraq (in the Iraq War). Shortly after graduating from high school (Shaw High School, in East Cleveland, Ohio, 1998), Michael began his military career in the United States Army, having completed ROTC training while in high school.

Before deploying for the first of his many tours of duty during his military career that began in 1998, our son displayed a degree and a sense of wisdom far beyond his eighteen years of age. I'll never forget the day of what I still refer to as the day of the "dreadful conversation."

It (the conversation) began this way as "Mike" pulled me and his mom aside one day for the conversation, which also was a reality check for each of us.

"Mom, Dad," he said, "You both need to know some important details about me being in active duty as I am subject to being in any place in the world in harm's way. If one day a white, unmarked car pulls up to the house and two soldiers emerge from it, they are probably going to bring you news about four possible outcomes of things that could have happened to me.

I could be a prisoner of war, I could have been shot (injured) in the line of duty, I could be MIA (Missing In Action), or I could be dead." We sat in somber silence for what seemed to be an eternity—though it was just a matter of about five minutes.

Breaking the silence, I responded to my son. "We really don't want to hear about what might happen to you when you deploy, but it is something that we need to know. Remember, we love you, but more importantly, God loves you, and you are in His hands wherever you go, and whatever happens to you."

Nineteen years after this conversation (in 1998), on January 23, 2007, this scenario unfolded in "real time" just like our son Michael explained to us it would. My wife Valerie telephoned me on that fateful day while I was conducting Bible Study at our church when the call came.

This conversation ensued. My wife said to me, "You need to come home as soon as possible because the kitchen sink has sprung a leak, and the plumber (Victor) is on his way to fix it.

My response was, "We are just wrapping up Bible Study, and I'll be home in about fifteen minutes."

My wife, growing a bit impatient, called me a second time. "Where are you?"

"I'm right in front of the house now," I reported, "but I can't get into the driveway because there is a car blocking my path." All I noticed about this "mystery car" is that it was "unmarked" and parked in front of my house, on the wrong side of the street.

As I exited my car and made my way up the front stairs of my house, the scenario that my son (Michael) shared with my wife and me at the time he entered active duty in the United States Army in 1998, eerily unfolded in front of me. At the entrance of my front door stood two soldiers, representatives of the United States Army.

These two soldiers began to share with me the best of their information and knowledge about the events leading up to my son's death in Iraq. All I can recall is their opening words.

"We are sad to inform you, Mr. Wiggins, that your son, Staff Sergeant Michael J. Wiggins, lost his life on January 23, 2007, and is officially a casualty of War."

As I shared on numerous occasions with friends and strangers alike, those words struck me in the head like a "left-right combination" of punches from heavyweight boxing champion Mike Tyson. I fell to the floor muttering some form of unintelligible words sprinkled with sobs and moans of intense agony and pain that I have never experienced before in my life, and by the grace of God will never experience again.

A few moments later, my daughter Nichole began comforting and hugging me, sharing words that I will never forget that at once seemed to calm my spirit and revive my grieving soul

"Dad," she said, "it's only a test from God, He's testing our faith!"

It goes without saying, but my daughter's words were not only accurate, but they were also prophetically correct. These past eighteen years that have passed since Mike's tragic death have been a test of my family's faith in God.

Beginning on January 23, 2007, my wife and I have experienced what I can only describe as "a living hell." For me personally, (my wife and daughter both processed this experience differently from me), the first six-month period after our great loss, there were endless days and nights of weeping and shedding of tears, only intermittently separated by sleepless days and nights.

I don't recall eating or sleeping, having much care or concern about anything. No, nothing! It was just like being lost in a deep, dark tunnel, which seemed to have no way out. At other times, it was just like not being able to swim, while at the same time not being able to drown.

As the senior pastor of a church in Cleveland, Ohio (Friends Fellowship Bible Church), I never missed a Sunday morning preaching from the pulpit about a God who, during this time, I felt had abandoned me and distanced Himself from me.

The day after my son Michael died, I called my job (I was at that time teaching seventh and eighth grade math) to inform my supervisor about my loss. My principal's words to me, which I took literally, were, "Mr. Wiggins, I can only imagine what you and your family must be going through. Take as much time off as you would like or need."

For the next three months, until after Spring Break in April of 2007, I was not in the classroom teaching. When I did return to my classroom, just a few weeks before the school year of 2006–2007 ended, I merely went through the motions and don't remember teaching anything. I just didn't care.

Thank God my students understood and never bothered me for the duration of the school year!

During the time of my grieving process, I believe that I was led by the Spirit of God to read King David's account of his experience of losing his son after a time of sickness (2nd Samuel 12:16–23). This eye-opening passage of the scripture says that David, during the proceedings that culminated in the death of his infant son, didn't eat or sleep, lay prostrate before the Lord's presence night and day, grieving, crying, and praying until the child died. (v.19)

After a period of time (when the child died), David arose from his time of hopelessness and despair, washed and anointed himself, changed his clothes, began to eat, and even worshiped the Lord (v. 20–23).

My time of prolonged grieving and going through much the same experiences as David ended when my good friend (the late Ed Coles) took me to a night of praise and worship, which Joel Osteen hosted in Cleveland, Ohio.

Personally, I am not (now or then) a big fan or supporter of Joel Osteen, but the message he shared at this specific time in my life still resonates in my soul today.

He (Joel Osteen) spoke about how and where we go after we have endured great personal losses in our lives. Wow! This message was tailor-made for me! It was a powerful, heart-changing, soul-searching message that spoke directly to me.

Just like King David in this text referenced above, "I arose from the stupor of my self-initiated circumstances, washed my face, changed my clothes, and began to eat and sleep again. I then sought out, with a clean, clear, renewed, and refreshed heart and mind, a time of praising and worshipping God!

Ever so slowly, my perspective about what I had endured began to change, and I was finding peace amid my great loss! From the depths of my heart and soul, I was able to proclaim: "But thanks be to God! Who gives us the victory through our Lord and Savior Jesus Christ!" (1st Corinthians 15:57)

Because of the power of God that I have available to me through the finished work of Jesus Christ on the cross of Calvary, I expected to win this battle over grief, pain, hopelessness, helplessness, and loneliness—and by that same power I am destined to keep on winning over the challenges of life!

Just like He (Jesus Christ) has promised me and you, I have "come unto him" in times of being burdened down and heavy laden and have found and experienced the rest that only He gives (Matthew 11:28–30). This rest for my soul has eased my yoke and caused my burdens to be light.

Living through and experiencing the death of a child brings a degree of pain that I have never been able to put into words. We (my wife and I) had so many plans, dreams, hopes, and aspirations about what we envisioned our son Michael was going to accomplish in his lifetime.

On a cold, dreary Saturday afternoon, February 3, 2007, we laid our only son to rest in Lakeview Cemetery, just a few feet away from the final resting place of his grandmother (Gladys) and our illustrious former mayor of Cleveland, Ohio, Carl Stokes.

Even now, my son's final words to me in person ring out in my heart and mind loud and clear: "Don't worry, Dad, God will take care of me." Not only did Michael "expect" to win, he did! I am forever at peace with what God did in my son's short twenty-six-year life, and it is still working together for my good because I love the Lord and have been called according to His purpose (Romans 8:28).

As I continue in the journey of my life, I both accept and expect that there will be many more times and days of trouble as we struggle by and with the power of God to live a triumphant, victorious life. We don't like talking about this as a promise of God, but in this world in which we are living, there is going to be trouble (John 16:33).

The other part of this great promise is that even though we are going to experience difficulties and hardships, we are going to overcome because Christ, our Savior, has already overcome! It is this great promise of a secure and everlasting future that continues to encourage me and to propel me into what seems to be an unknown future by my own limited understanding, but one of unimaginable success if I stay the course and remain committed to following God's plan!!

Yes, I expect to win because I have been born again of God because of the finished work of Jesus Christ on the cross atoning for my sins. By faith, I have accepted Him. 1st John 5:4 tells us "That everyone born of God is going to overcome the world: and this is the victory that overcomes the world, even our faith." It's all about faith!

The success of this entire Christian life in which we are living (you and I as believers) comes down to the question of our faith. We know that faith is the gift of God that led to our Salvation (Ephesians 2:8–9). Having faith in God means that we trust in the truth of His promises and are willing to rely upon Him for love, for guidance, for strength, and for His power.

Even when it appears that the enemy is "stacked against us," **I still expect to win.**

Because of this faith again, we come to believe that God will and has worked His redemptive plan out in our lives even as we contend with our own challenging situations and circumstances.

For the past five-plus years, I have been praying for God to send me some help in shepherding our church (Friends Fellowship Bible Church in Cleveland, Ohio). Our ministry began modestly in the front living room of my home

(13900 Potomac Avenue) in East Cleveland, Ohio, on the first Sunday in January of 2006.

The previous twenty-year period, from 1988 until 2006, I faithfully served as the Assistant Pastor of the Bright Star Missionary Baptist Church under the pastorate of Rev. Dr. David Hunter. It was during this transitional time of "firsthand training and on-the-job experience" that I learned and applied most of the practical nuances of the pastoral ministry.

During this time of invaluable training (by the grace of God), I was blessed to graduate from Moody Bible Institute in 1988, and to finally go on to complete both my master's degree and doctorate degrees in Theology from the Master's Seminary in Evansville, Indiana, in 2004 and 2004, respectively! Truly, God is good and continues to manifest Himself in my life today.

After much prayer and seeking God's plan and will for my life, I was led by the Spirit of God to begin my present-day ministry (launching of the Friends Fellowship Bible Church) in January of 2006 with twelve (12) committed and devoted members.

It was from this group gathering of what I affectionately referred to as "The Circle of Friends" that we named our church "The Friends Fellowship Bible Church." (Proverbs 17:17: "A friend loves at all times, and a brother is born for adversity"). The name of our church was in honor of these "special friends," taking upon themselves the awesome financial cost of paying for my seminary training!

Without their god-led and directed support of love for what God allowed them to see in me, I probably would not be Rev. Dr. Anthony J. Wiggins today! It is no small wonder that I expect to win, and because of God's goodness, love, and mercy, I am winning! **The best is yet to come!**

Throughout the now nineteen-year existence of our church, we have had a time of modest success, a series of challenging and trying times, yet we continue to weather the storm of spreading the Word of God to a lost and dying world of sinners who need to hear it. It hasn't been easy, but God has sustained us.

Pastoring a church—regardless of how large or small it is—presents a unique challenge for us as we (pastors) try to blend hearts, minds, and different ideas of ministry into one common united purpose—getting the Word of God out to people near and far as we have been called and mandated to do by God Himself (Matthew 28:19–20—go therefore and teach all nations, as God has commanded us. Jesus promises to be with us even unto the end of the world). **We are going to win!**

Over the course of the past five or six years, I have been praying to God, asking Him to send me some help in the day-to-day administration and operations of our church, from preaching to teaching, to pastoring, to mentoring, to just handling the daily affairs and business of the church. Additionally, remember that for two years, COVID shut us down, and we were not even allowed to meet publicly!

We (as a church family) have witnessed at least five strategic leaders of our ministry transitioning and going home to be with the Lord during this time. Yet, God has still blessed and sustained us to carry on our ministry.

It is and has been quite a burden for me (a person) to carry the responsibility for this work alone. The answer to my prayer came just in the last week! (March 1, 2025) On that date, I was proud to present to our church my new assistant pastor! (Tyrone Dorsey)

In His own way as well as in His own time, God does answer prayer! Many members of our congregation were quick to chime in with their initial assessment of the immediate changes that have taken place in our ministry.

They in unison remarked, "It was a blessing to know that the tremendous burden of trying to carry out the overall program of our church in just the hands of our pastor (referring to me) has finally been lifted! We don't know, Pastor, how you were able to hold things together by yourself, but thank God you were able to do so and did!"

Assistant Pastor Tyrone Dorsey literally "hit the ground running," and we are well on our way with plans regrouping, reorganizing, and strategically putting things in place for the advancement of our church ministry!

Not only did we expect to win, but we did, and **the best is yet to come** as we continue to trust the direction that God has put in place for us in advancing His kingdom here on earth!

There, of course, were times that I wanted to quit, to give up, but realizing and knowing that God is faithful to each and every one of His promises, and will still continue to supply us with all that we need in order to ensure that His message of love, hope, and Salvation through Jesus Christ reaches to all the ends of the earth.

It is the love of God that guarantees victory for us over all things opposing us during our lives. His Word (Romans 8:37) tells us that "we are more than conquerors because God Himself loves us." With Him on our side and in our lives, we will be victorious.

We have this confidence in God because by and through His power we have the ability to do all things (Philippians 4:13). True and lasting victory in our lives is not just limited to our worldly accomplishments, but it also includes us being able to overcome personal struggles, the ability to stand firm in our faith throughout our trials, and living lives that commit themselves to pleasing God in all things that we do.

I'll never be able to thank God enough for all that He has done for me, all that He is doing right now, and all that I am claiming that He has yet to do for me in the days and years that I have not yet even experienced.

Just knowing, believing, and saying that "God is good," never quite expresses the magnitude or the depth of what I personally feel for a God who has never shown anything to me (or any of us) other than an unconditional love despite the fact that this love was and has been extended towards us even while we yet were sinners (Romans 5:8).

"But thanks be to God, who always leads us to triumph in Christ, and manifests through us the sweet aroma of the knowledge of him in every place." (2nd Corinthians 2:14). Because of this truth, regardless of what we have and will experience in our lives, I expect to win! There is a winner in me! Is there one in you?

CHAPTER TWELVE
"WHERE DO WE GO FROM HERE?"

"There isn't any temptation that you have experienced that is unusual for humans. God, who faithfully keeps his promises, will not allow you to be tempted beyond your power to resist. But when you are tempted, he will also give you the ability to endure the temptation as your way of escape."
(1st Corinthians 10:13, GWT)

After we (particularly us as Christians) have gone through the challenges of a lifetime of seasons or times of trials, adversities, difficulties, frustrations, hopelessness, and despair of every kind, the obvious questions to consider are: **"Where do we go from here? How do we keep moving forward with hope?"**

The phrase **"Where do we go from here?"** ironically is the title of the fourth and final book written by the late Civil Rights leader and Nobel Prize winner Dr. Martin Luther King, Jr. (1967) in response to his views and observations about the progress and or the success, failures, and the hopes of the civil rights movement in the United States—which he led until his death by assassination in 1968.

King noted in 1967 that the "sagging walls of segregation" were beginning to come tumbling down, but still much work needed to be done to advance the causes of not just black people in the United States, but for people of all races and cultures who, for hundreds of years, had been marginalized and treated unfairly and unjustly.

Sad to say, but many of these injustices still exist today in 2025, but King was always hopeful and prayerfully optimistic that conditions (too numerous to mention) would change, and he gave his life fighting to do so.

For us as Christians, the hope that we have for not only our present and more importantly our future lives, rests in the "unfailing, unchanging, all-powerful, eternal hands of our Lord and Savior, Jesus Christ! There is no hope beyond the hope that we have in Jesus Christ.

Nothing that we have gone through or experienced in our lives should ever be misconstrued as unusual because God Himself has forewarned us that in this world in which we live, there are always going to be trials as well as tribulations and troubles of all kinds (John 16:33).

God's promise is that even though we must contend with a world of challenges, we will ultimately overcome because our Lord Himself has already "overcome" all obstacles that might and will come before us and has emerged victoriously over them all!—even ultimately death itself, our greatest enemy and challenge. This is the foundation of the eternal hope that we have.

This fact alone answers the questions of **"Where do we go from here, and how do we move forward with hope?"** Personally, I have found that the only "place to go" or to turn to that will ensure me with a sense of hope that will never fail, is in Jesus Christ! In Him there is no failure, so by going to Him and trusting in Him, my hope is steadfast, and my future is secure.

On the day that I (and hopefully each of you) received my (our) Salvation in, through, and because of the finished work of Jesus Christ on the cross, the guarantee of my (our) present and more importantly future disposition was assured and completed.

"Where do we go from here?" Psalm 121:1–8 proclaims my course of action, which is my confidence that everything in my life will be alright: I will lift my eyes to the hills, which is where the source of all my strength, my hope, and my help originates. The Lord himself is my provider, my keeper, my sustainer throughout the entirety of my life. He is the lifter of my bowed-down head and my sometimes-weak countenance. He is the only one alone who can give me the assurance of a present and a future of perfect hope, rest, and peace. Because of this, I can rejoice amid all adversity and trials of every type that have and will come my way.

The words from an old song that I learned (and sang) many years ago in the days of my youth, echo from within the depths of my soul: "Where can I go, where can I go, needing a refuge for my soul, needing a friend, to be with me 'til the end, where can I go but to the Lord!"

I continuously thank and praise God for allowing me the privilege of being raised in a home and an environment where the Word of God and the principles of Jesus Christ were always presented as the solution and the answer to all the problems that I would ever face throughout my lifetime!

Everywhere in front of me (in the presence of my parents, my uncles and aunts, and extended members of my church family), I saw living examples of what true, dedicated Christian role models were like, and thank God for the impact that this has had upon solidifying my faith and belief in Him, even until this present time in my life!

Truly, this has been the "glue" that has held me together amid an ever-changing, unstable, ungodly world. Without this foundation built upon Jesus Christ, I most assuredly would not have made it this far. Life continues to be a challenge every day, but I have confidence and the peace that passes all understanding in knowing the way to go!

Not only can I move forward in the light of an everlasting hope that is rooted and sustained by faith in Jesus Christ, but also God's Word promises me the only real key to prosperity and good success.

For me, prosperity and success are not measured by the thoughts, the ideas, and the principles of the messages of the many so-called "prosperity preachers" of today, and I won't call any of them by name because I don't sit in the seat of judgment of their philosophies or beliefs in the messages that they preach.

However, I do believe that there is much more to the Christian life than to measure one's success or the fact that God has shown favor upon them because of the size of their church, the dimensions of the homes in which they live, the ridiculous cost of the cars that they drive, or the expensive clothes that they wear.

The late Dr. J. Vernon McGhee in my estimation summed it up best in response to the preaching and the teaching of the popular "prosperity theology" being promoted today: (this is not a direct quote but a paraphrase of my thoughts about what he suggests or believes) "Any man growing rich off of the preaching, the teaching, and the declaration of the Word of God and the ministry of spreading the gospel of Jesus Christ, has lost sight of or has abandoned his true calling."

We all must one day stand before God to give an account of why and how we did what we did as we labored to accomplish our one ultimate goal or calling from God to advance the kingdom of God by winning, gaining, and adding souls to the kingdom of God, the message that Salvation only comes through a personal relationship of faith and belief in Jesus Christ. Nothing else is going to matter!

A good friend of mine and a dear sister in Christ, as well as a staunch believer and supporter of our ministry for many years, Ernestine Pace, sums up that the entirety of who and what we are can only be measured by what we do best by this statement: **"Pastor, let the main thing be the main thing!"**

In the more than forty years that I have labored in the ministry of spreading the gospel since "answering the call," I have tried to the best of my ability to "let the main thing be the main thing," which without a question or a doubt, is spreading and sharing the redemptive message of the gospel of Jesus Christ—that only through accepting, believing, and trusting in him can we find eternal hope, rest, and peace for our souls!

I have found that (in our churches today) too much time, energy, emphasis, and effort have been placed on things that simply don't matter when it comes down to the reality of what our Christian faith is all about.

Whether or not I wear a suit and a tie to worship service on Sunday morning, (men) or a nice Sunday suit or dress with an adorning hat or a matching purse (women), whether or not I join the "Mother's Board or the Missionary Society" and wear a white suit every first Sunday of the month have nothing to do with Salvation that is by and through confessing Jesus Christ as my Lord and Savior!

A dressed-up outer appearance says little or nothing about what really matters, which is the content as well as the character of your heart. "Man looks on the outward appearance, while God is more concerned about our heart." (1st Samuel 16:7)

In our dress as well as in our deportment, we should present ourselves respectfully in the presence of God and each other. **"Where do we go from here?"** We go forward with the mindset as well as the heart in knowing that God wants us to "redeem the time," because the days in which we are living are full of evil, wickedness, contention, and strife (Ephesians 5:16).

There is still much work for us to do, and time is of great essence, and should be our priority and our concern when it comes to the things of God**. "Where do we go from here?"**

Ironically, again, the great late civil rights leader, Rev. Dr. Martin Luther King Jr., stated in a sermon entitled **"Where do we go from here?"** delivered in Atlanta, Georgia, at the annual conference of the Southern Christian Leadership Council **(SCLC)** in 1967:

"Now, a lot of us are preachers. And all of us have our moral convictions and concerns. And so often we have problems with power. But there is nothing wrong with power if power is used correctly.

"You see, what happened is that some of our philosophers got off base, and one of the great problems of history is that the concepts of love and power have usually been contrasted as opposites, polar opposites, so that love is identified with a resignation of power, and power with a denial of love.

"It was this same misinterpretation that caused the great philosopher Nietzsche, who was a philosopher of the will to power, to reject the Christian concept of love.

"It was this same misinterpretation that caused Christian theologians to reject Nietzsche's philosophy of the will to power in the name of the Christian idea of love. Now we gotta get this thing right. What is needed is the realization that power without love is reckless and abusive, and that love without power is sentimental and anemic.

"Power, at its best—power, at its best, is love, implementing the demands of justice, and justice at its best is love correcting everything that stands against love—and this is what we must see as we move on."

"Where do we go from here?" We move on and go forward in spreading and promoting the truth of the power of God-led, guided, and directed by his love. Jesus Christ Himself emphatically states in Matthew 25:40, "What you have done to the least of them, you have also in effect and actuality, done the same to me."

The love of God must, above all else, be dispensed and shared with people everywhere, regardless of their "lack" of position or status in the world in which we live. All too often, we exclude that vast part of the people of our world and our society that have been "marginalized and consequently forgotten." The mandate of the "Great Commission" (Matthew 28:19–20) given to us by our Lord and Savior Jesus Christ commands and compels us to take the gospel message into all the world, teaching, preaching, and making disciples of all people!

Sadly, as we get caught up in "the traditions of man," we lose sight of what our purpose is today relative to who and what God has called us to be and to do, which is to be the "beacon of hope" shining the light along the path of the way of the darkness that so many lost souls are stumbling around in that they might see their way from despair to the light.

"Where do we go from here?" We should go forward with all diligence and perseverance to fulfill the mandate that we have been given in and through Jesus Christ that hearts, minds, and lives might be changed forever through the power of God.

When it comes down to where we are going in our spiritual lives, I believe that we are left with three possible choices or courses of action to take. First, we can make the choice to do nothing by simply deciding to stay where we are.

Our second choice that we can make is to "backtrack" or go in the opposite direction to which we are heading and give up ground, or finally, we can decide to move forward and grow by continuing to trust in God and believe that He will lead, guide, and direct us in the way that we should go until we accomplish that which He has set in front of us.

Finally, the third and final choice that we can make suggests to us that if we commit ourselves to trusting God, we can move forward in faith, trusting and believing that because of the presence of God in our lives, we can and shall be able to succeed and accomplish greater things for the cause of Jesus Christ!

1st Corinthians 2:9 prophetically encourages us that "no eye anywhere has ever seen, no ear anywhere has even begun to hear, and no heart anywhere can even perceive or even begin to understand that which God has prepared for those of us who love and serve him!"

This promise gives me the continued hope as well as the strength, the power, and the ability to keep putting forth the best that is in me to accomplish the work that God has called me to do**. "Where do we go from here?"**

We (I) continue to move forward against all odds and that which tries to hinder or block my path from the calling of that which God has on my life. Philippians 1:6 continues to further encourage me that "He which has begun a good work in me (which is what God has done in me and in you) will continue to perform that work in us until the day of Jesus Christ."

The best is yet to come! I believe it because God said it, I expect it because God promised it, and I look forward to receiving it just as God has predestined and ordained that it would happen for me in all that I endeavor to do in advancing the kingdom of God. What about you???

CHAPTER THIRTEEN
"THE BEST IS YET TO COME"

"Forget the former things, do not dwell on the past. See, I am doing a new thing! Now it springs up, do you not perceive it? I am making a way in the wilderness and streams in the wasteland."
(Isaiah 43:18–19 NIV)

After a bit of research, I discovered that the popular phrase **"the best is yet to come"** was a 1959 song composed by Cy Coleman, a jazz pianist and songwriter, and recorded by the late great singer Frank Sinatra on one of his albums in 1964. In fact, this song was the last song that Sinatra sang publicly on February 25, 1995, and those iconic words **(The Best Is Yet To Come)** were etched on his original tombstone when he died (though it was later changed to reflect a different message).

This phrase also has a place as a quote from the poet Robert Browning in a poem: "Grow old along with me! The best is yet to be, the last of life, for which the first was made. Our times are in his hands who saith a whole I planned, youth shows but half, trust God, nor be afraid."

In this quote by Robert Browning, I believe that he is further alluding to the idea of expressing that the essence of life is found in hopeful anticipation, accompanied by the reality of a lifelong companionship with someone. He challenges the philosophy that perhaps the most challenging and rewarding times in our lives, which we can benefit from, would be the hope and the possibility of that which we might have in the days that we have yet to experience in the future.

"The best is yet to come." From our Christian perspective, "the best is yet to come" can be viewed by us as followers of Jesus Christ, as our ultimate reward simply lies in the realization of sharing eternal life with God in heaven, which is, for us as Christians, our ultimate destination. One such assurance that the best is yet to come can be found in understanding God's Word (John 14:2–3): "In my Father's house there are many mansions," Jesus says.

The fact that He (Jesus) has gone away to prepare a place for us (believers, like no place we have ever witnessed) is the assurance that when He comes back, and He will, He will take us to be with Him forever. This new place awaiting us in heaven will be free from pain, sin, death, and even hell itself.

God is always (during the time of our lives) shaping and preparing us to be the recipients of greater things. He is the author of great things! This phrase also ensures us of hope far away and above that which we presently have in this world today.

It goes without saying that we (as Christians) are always going to experience our fair share of trying times accompanied by a series of events that could shatter our faith in God if we allow them to dominate and control our lives. God never promised us lives that would be free from challenges and troubles just because we believe and trust in Him. Ultimately, He promises us victory and success in all that we do (1st Corinthians 15:57).

Quite the opposite, we are told that in this present world in which we are living, we should expect trials, troubles, hardships, and difficulties (John 16:33). God's promise remains that even in these trying times, we will be able to endure and to overcome, because He (our Lord and Savior) has already overcome.

Recently, as we came to the end of the past year (2024), it was filled with great promises and the hope of good things to come in the new year. However, our family was faced with what can best be termed as life-changing events. My sister-in-law (Sharon, my wife's sister), who had lived with us for about ten years, suffered a stroke shortly after moving into her own apartment.

The greatest challenge that we (my wife and I) faced at this time was obviously a monumental challenge for us: "Who was going to be there to care for Sharon as she began the tedious journey of physically trying to put her life back together?" We thank God that the prognosis of her regaining her health and strength was good, because although the stroke left her partially paralyzed on her left side, it could have been a lot worse.

My wife, as she has done for virtually all of her sister Sharon's life, immediately went into a "protective caregiver mode" and began from day one to provide her sister with day-to-day support that was much needed, without any hesitation or reservation about her own well-being.

My wife (Valerie) and I both have full-time jobs, but as we concluded our work schedules for each day, we would spend an additional four to five hours daily physically supporting Sharon with all that she needed (from cooking and preparing meals, to washing her clothes and even providing assistance to physically walk).

Additionally, on each weekend, my wife would "physically move" into her sister's apartment from Friday night until coming back home on Sunday evening to prepare for her job the next day. This routine continued for just about three months (from December 2024 until March 2025), and periodically, I would mention to my wife that after a while, "even iron will wear out." Sad to say it, but my words were ominously true and came to pass.

Over the duration of these three months, I watched my wife literally pour out her heart, her soul, her mind, and her physical support, and even her finances, to help restore some semblance of order to her sister's life. Then, as if on cue, the "whispers" began to come from me and all of our closest friends and relatives who were privy to the situation. "Val (my wife) is going to wear herself out."

Periodically, from time to time, my wife intimated to all of us: "I am tired, in fact, I am exhausted." A preliminary evaluation by our neighbor, Dr. Kyle Black, in his estimation, suggested that Valerie was suffering from a condition known as "Caregiver's Fatigue." He suggested that she rest for a few days (which she did), and if she wasn't better, we should seek out further medical support and assistance.

Then seemingly out of nowhere, the inevitable happened, which would change our lives in a way that we would have never imagined. As my wife and I concluded our normal workday, we received a call from Fred (my sister-in-law's boyfriend) with his usual standard message. "What time are you guys coming over to help with Sharon?"

I looked at my wife, tired, physically depleted, and exhausted after a strenuous three-month period of giving support to her sister, and heard her response. "Fred, I'm not coming over today to help Sharon. In fact, I don't know when I will be able to help. I'm tired and need to take care of myself. I just can't do it anymore!"

The next few moments (experienced over a few short days) I will never forget. I literally had to take my wife by hand, and with one arm around her waist, help her up the stairs to physically put her in bed. She "crashed" off to sleep for what seemed to be days that never ended. She only woke up long enough to call her job, requesting to take a few days off.

Fortunately, my wife has been on her job for over thirty-seven years and has amassed a countless number of "sick days" and "vacation time." The Saturday morning that she woke up (I'll never forget), she had but one request from me that struck me to the core of my heart.

"Tony," she said, "could you help me get out of bed? I can't move."

"What do you mean you can't move?" I said, shocked and astonished.

"No, I can't," was her reply.

Thank God that our godson, Jeremiah, had recently come to live with us for a few months, and with his help, we gingerly assisted my wife in her movements from room to room throughout the house.

After a few days of assisting my wife back and forth in this manner just to move around the house, I persuaded her that it was indeed time for us to seek out medical assistance and get some type of evaluation about her health. After arriving at the emergency room of the Cleveland Clinic (March 12th, 2025), who had to transport her by ambulance, we waited for the eternity of a few hours before my wife's health was evaluated.

Finally, Valerie (my wife) was admitted as a patient, and for the next seven or eight days, countless tests were conducted to determine the cause as well as the extent of her condition.

Our faith in God has been and is being tested in ways that we have never realized before, and after about a two-week stay in The Cleveland Clinic, my wife was released and admitted to The Cleveland Clinic Rehabilitation Hospital to continue her recovery from what we still don't exactly know.

Presently, as we approached the end of March 2025, my wife's progress to recovery had been slow, and for our entire family, it had been quite a challenge and a struggle.

In our nearly forty-seven years of marriage, my wife and I have never suffered any type of sickness, illness, or health concerns other than a cold or the flu! For that, we give thanks and praise to God. As we deal with my wife's present health issues and concerns, I must confess that this is new territory and a new challenge for us.

However, as people of faith in God, we know that everything that is happening to us in this present predicament and struggle, according to God's Word (Romans 8:28), is working together for our good. This principle and truth from God's Word has been and is a hard truth to accept, but God is in control and knows what He is doing even though we don't.

I must confess that many times in our lives (especially right now), we find ourselves in situations that cause us to question God because we simply have no insight, understanding, or even a clue about what He is doing, or why He is allowing the things that are happening right now to happen.

As I continue writing this book, my wife (Valerie) is presently completing a twelve-day "stay" at the Cleveland Clinic Rehabilitation, dealing with health issues and concerns that seem to have mysteriously appeared in her life because of the physical, mental, and emotional fatigue she experienced while supporting her sister (Sharon) in her recovery from a debilitating stroke.

She has been diagnosed with a condition known as "peripheral neuropathy," which is a condition or a disease that causes some damage or interference to the central nervous system, resulting in tingling sensations and weakness in the arms, legs, and hands (and possibly diabetes).

The prescribed treatment for this condition is rest, along with some adjoining medications needed to control it, and prayerfully and hopefully, arrest and reverse its effect upon her body. Over the course of the next few days, my wife, by the grace of God, is scheduled to be released from the rehabilitation hospital to continue her road to recovery at home (April 6, 2025).

For my family and me, this is and continues, at this present moment, to be a very challenging time in our lives as we commit and devote every effort, along with our prayers, for Valerie's full and complete recovery and restoration of her health.

We claim every promise of God, and we know and believe that He is in control of and in charge of everything that happens in our lives, and that it is all working together for our good—just as the Word of God proclaims (Romans 8:28).

Finally, we know that the way forward and the path to recovery for my wife and our family is going to be challenging, long, and difficult. There is only one promise of God that dominates our lives and gives us peace of mind in all that we are encountering or have yet to contend with: The Best Is Yet to Come!

By faith, I continue to hold fast and true to the promises that God has given to me, found in countless passages of Scripture in His Word.

Throughout all that has happened to me and my family during our lives, (both the good and the bad) we have been able to "weather and to withstand the storms of life" because we rest assured and confident in God's faithful and eternal promise that "He would not put more upon us in terms of trials and tribulations than we are able to bear." (1st Corinthians 10:13)

In the midst of all that "has been placed upon us" we know that God Himself, because of His love for us and that He is attuned to everything that affects us in life, will give us the grace, the love, and the mercy to bear our trials (whatever they might be) by providing a way for us to escape our situation and present afflictions! His grace is sufficient!

Although this time of challenge and testing may be unique to my family and me, we realize and understand that we are not alone in this struggle, and that countless other believers (and nonbelievers alike) are also, even at this very moment, experiencing similar situations.

Let me further offer words of encouragement first to myself and then to anyone facing difficult moments in their own lives where their faith and resolve are being challenged and tested by God (1st Peter 1:6–7, New Living Translation).

"So be truly glad. There is wonderful joy ahead, even though you must endure many trials for a little while. These trials will show that your faith is genuine. It is being tested as fire tests and purifies gold, though your faith is far more precious than mere gold. So when your faith remains strong through many trials, it will bring you much praise and glory and honor on the day when Jesus is revealed to the whole world."

Inevitably, we are all going to be tested by various trials in our lives, but remember that there is great value in faith that is tested because God Himself is at work in our lives, and will "prove Himself" to us as well as give us the love, the patience, the support, and the endurance to not allow these tests to overcome us by weakening our faith. As we continue to commit ourselves to Him time after time again, we ultimately will come to realize that in Him and through Him, the best is yet to come, and I, by faith in God, stand open, ready, willing, and expecting to receive the full benefit of all the blessings that He has for me!

EPILOGUE

"However, as it is written: what no eye has seen, what no ear has heard, and what no human mind has conceived—The things God has prepared for those who love him."
(1st Corinthians 2:9, NIV)

Personally, I love the Contemporary English Version's (CEV) translation of the passage of scripture found in Job 8:7, which says: **"Your future will be brighter by far than your past."** This gives me a sense of hope and that the future unfolding before me holds great promise.

Without a doubt, God, through His Holy Spirit, gave me the title of this book **(The Best Is Yet To Come)** which conveys the idea and the thought that after many years of laboring and toiling for what seemed at times to yield, in my way of thinking, little or no measurable signs of progress or success, that brighter days indeed are ahead of me and what I am striving to do for the kingdom of God, **the best is yet to come!**

One of my favorite passages of scripture that I have for many years held near and dear to my heart (Philippians 1:6) confidently reassures me of an amazing promise and truth: **He (God) that began a good work in you (and in me) will continue to perform that work in and through us until it is completed at the day of Jesus Christ. I thank and praise God that He is not through with us yet!**

The "good work" that was established and begun in me and in the lives of every other believer was the redemptive work of Salvation, as well as the call and the implementation of working to spread the gospel of faith in Jesus Christ to a lost and dying world of sinners until the return of our Lord Himself. I am convinced and believe that there is no greater call anywhere.

It is this "good work" that I have been called to, and as I press forward to accomplish all that God has set before me, I have struggled and fallen (many of us have and will). Sometimes the way was not so clear or so bright, but by God's grace and power, I have pushed on. Truly, I anticipate and expect God to do greater things in my life, not just for me personally, but for the cause of Jesus Christ!

Consequently, I can rejoice and give thanks because **the best is yet to come. My future is already much brighter than my past has ever been!**

Proverbs 24:26 makes the declaration that a just or righteous man (person) will fall seven times, but because of the grace of God, which gives him strength and perseverance, he will rise and continue in the course of his journey and his calling.

Over the course of the last few years (I won't say how many), I have literally spent time engaged in juggling multiple "jobs" and "careers" from being the owner/operator of a day-care center, being a pastor of a church, being an educator of junior high school as well as high school students, serving as a hospice pastor and chaplain, to teaching courses of theology at a local Bible college! Only by the grace of God have I been able to effectively maintain each of these "jobs" without succumbing to the pressure that each brings, respectively.

It would be remiss for me to say that I haven't enjoyed each position thoroughly, and have found them to be both rewarding and fulfilling, but in some way, they have hindered and obstructed me from devoting myself to what God has truly called and ordained me to pursue; the commitment to spreading the gospel of Jesus Christ in ministry to a lost and dying world through the teaching and the preaching of His Word!

As the end of March 2025 was approaching, and after a time of prayerfully considering exactly the direction God Himself wanted me to pursue (though I always knew), I made the decision to "give up" my career as an educator of high school students, to pursue ministry completely pastoring and building our church, and preaching and teaching the Word of God primarily and exclusively for the rest of my life that God has given me!

Truly, I am expecting God to do great and amazing things in and through my ministry as I further yield and submit myself to be more open, receptive, responsive, and available to His direction, His leading, and His calling. **The best is yet to come,** and I know that God is clearly directing my path. I have come too far to turn around!

This year (2025) marks the nineteenth year (beginning in January, 2006) since I answered the call by God to begin the work of our church (Friends Fellowship Bible Church) with twelve faithfully committed and dedicated friends and a few family members in the front living room of our modest former home (my wife Valerie and I) at 13900 Potomac Avenue in East Cleveland, Ohio.

It was by faith in God that these twelve friends whom I have dubbed "The Circle of Friends," were led by the Lord to fund the cost and the entire expense of my seminary education, allowing me to earn both my Master of Theology and my Doctorate of Theology from Master's International University of Divinity (MIUD) in Evansville, Indiana (2004 2005, respectively).

I will forever be thankful and grateful to God for the unselfish effort and support of these twelve very special people in my life, for the great act of kindness and love extended to me. In honor of their support and love for me, I was proud to name our newly formed church after them! (Friends Fellowship Bible Church in 2006)

Over the time of our church's history, which has now, by the grace of God, spanned nineteen years, at least eight of the original "twelve Circle of Friends" remain as a part of our church today and support it wholeheartedly! (Ernestine and Ronald Pace, Viola Henderson, Ionia Bryson, my daughter Nichole Wiggins-Caliph, my wife Valerie Wiggins, Berniece Smith, and Ulysses Lewis)

(The others we have lost sadly in death as they have transitioned to the eternal presence of God—Emma Barnett, Charles Henderson Sr., James Sanders, and Carol Lewis, and Ed Coles)

We proudly refer to our church as a "purpose-driven church on the move serving the Lord," and hold fast to the principles and ideology found in Proverbs 17:17: **"A friend loves at all times, but a brother is born for**

adversity." We firmly believe that God has called and ordained us to band together in a spirit of unity, love, and undying support for each other.

Also, and more importantly, we are equally proud to be known as "a small church with a big heart." Throughout our history as a church, we have fed and clothed the hungry in the city and on the streets of Cleveland, Ohio, offered and given support to children in local city schools with books, clothing for the winter months, and toys for Christmas, subsidized rent assistance for many, and provided college tuition assistance for our young people aspiring to better themselves with higher education! As God has given to us, we continue to commit ourselves to blessing others. I believe that this is why we have survived while so many other churches have folded up and closed their doors.

Trusting and believing in God by activating our faith in Him, **the best is yet to come** as we continue to look forward with expectation and anticipation of all that God is going to do with, through, in, and for us.

We claim and hold fast and true to the prophetic promise of 1st Corinthians 2:9: **"Eyes haven't seen, ears haven't heard, and our minds are not able to begin to conceive the things that God has prepared for us because we love him and have committed ourselves to work for him."**

Finally, as a word of encouragement to anyone reading this book who might have been and even still presently finds themselves struggling with God's plan and direction for their lives, know that as you continue to trust in God and follow His direction for your life, **your future will by far be brighter than your past, and the best is yet to come!**

AUTHOR BIO

Anthony J. Wiggins (B.S. Education, Ashland University; Master of Practical Ministry, Doctor of Practical Theology, Master's International University of Divinity (MIUD) Evansville, Indiana; presently serves as the Senior Pastor/ Founder of Friends Fellowship Bible Church, Cleveland, Ohio, is an instructor of Theology at Maranatha Bible College and Institute, Cleveland, Ohio; retired educator of Theology and Reading at Cleveland Central Catholic High School, Cleveland, Ohio, and serves as a Hospice Pastor/Chaplain for Adoration Hospice (Cleveland/Independence/Ashtabula, Ohio offices)